OLYMPIC PARK
3-B AMUSEMENTS
IRVINGTON, N. J.
15c TREASURE HUNT 15c
Children Under 12 Years
INTERNATIONAL TICKET COMPANY, NEWARK, N. J.
20760

OLYMPIC PARK
3-B AMUSEMENTS
IRVINGTON, N. J.
9c MINIATURE TRAIN 9c
Children Under 12 Years
INTERNATIONAL TICKET COMPANY, NEWARK, N. J.
20760

OLYMPIC PARK
3-B AMUSEMENTS
IRVINGTON, N. J.
5c KIDDIE LAND 5c
Children under 12 Years
INTERNATIONAL TICKET COMPANY, NEWARK, N. J.
20754

OLYMPIC PARK
3-B AMUSEMENTS
IRVINGTON, N. J.
5c KIDDIE LAND 5c
Children under 12 Years
INTERNATIONAL TICKET COMPANY, NEWARK, N. J.
20754

OLYMPIC PARK
3-B AMUSEMENTS
IRVINGTON, N. J.
5c KIDDIE LAND 5c
Children under 12 Years
INTERNATIONAL TICKET COMPANY, NEWARK, N. J.
20754

OLYMPIC PARK
3-B AMUSEMENTS
IRVINGTON, N. J.
5c KIDDIE LAND 5c
Children under 12 Years
INTERNATIONAL TICKET COMPANY, NEWARK, N. J.
20754

OLYMPIC PARK
3-B AMUSEMENTS
IRVINGTON, N. J.
5c KIDDIE LAND 5c
Children under 12 Years
INTERNATIONAL TICKET COMPANY, NEWARK, N. J.
20754

OLYMPIC PARK
3-B AMUSEMENTS
IRVINGTON, N. J.
5c KIDDIE LAND 5c
Children under 12 Years
INTERNATIONAL TICKET COMPANY, NEWARK, N. J.
20754

Special Picnic
Combination Ticket
OLYMPIC PARK
IRVINGTON - MAPLEWOOD
Attached coupons Good on any Device
Good Only on Day Sold
1 coupon for any ride up to 15¢
2 coupons for any ride 20¢ or 25¢
3 coupons for any ride over 25¢
Price 70c

OLYMPIC PARK
GOOD FOR ONE RIDE
Not Good on Sundays or Holidays

TICKET
GOOD FOR RIDES ONLY
NOT REDEEMABLE X 097802

OLYMPIC PARK
IRVINGTON-MAPLEWOOD, N. J.
ONE TICKET 5c
GOOD FOR RIDES ONLY
NOT REDEEMABLE A 228417

OLYMPIC PARK
IRVINGTON-MAPLEWOOD, N. J.
ONE TICKET 5c
GOOD FOR RIDES ONLY
NOT REDEEMABLE A 228418

Olympic Park
SEASON
BUFFALO ELECTRIC PENNY GAME
This Coupon Entitles You to Merchandise
and must be redeemed not later than Labor Day!
71

2 Olympic Park 2
SKEE BALL
SAVE THESE COUPONS
They Are Redeemable For
VALUABLE PRIZES
Good Any Time
A

OLYMPIC PARK
IRVINGTON-MAPLEWOOD, N. J.
ONE TICKET
GOOD FOR RIDES ONLY
NOT REDEEMABLE X 097801

KIDDIE LAND
OLYMPIC PARK
10863
KIDDIE LAND
OLYMPIC PARK
10863

SMILE

A PICTURE HISTORY OF OLYMPIC PARK
1887 - 1965

ALAN A. SIEGEL

Rutgers University Press
New Brunswick, New Jersey

FIRST PUBLISHED BY THE IRVINGTON HISTORICAL SOCIETY, 1983

PUBLISHED BY RUTGERS UNIVERSITY PRESS,
NEW BRUNSWICK, NEW JERSEY, 1995

LIBRARY OF CONGRESS CATALOGING IN PUBLICATION DATA

Siegel, Alan A., 1939-
    Smile : a picture history of Olympic Park, 1887–1965 / Alan A.
Siegel.
        p. cm.
    Includes bibliographical references and index.
    ISBN 0-8135-2255-2
    1. Olympic Park (N.J.)—History. 2. New Jersey—Social life and
customs. 3. Olympic Park (N.J.)—History—Pictorial works. 4. New
Jersey—Social life and customs—Pictorial works. I. Title.
GV1853.3.N52S54 1995
791'.06'874931—dc20   95-11139

Picture credits—Grateful acknowledgment is made for permission to reproduce the
following photographs: Page 57, Edison National Historic Site; Pages 138, 139, from
"A Pictorial History of the Carousel," courtesy Frederick Fried; Pages 18, 70, Irvington
Free Public Library; Pages 39, 97, 102, North Jersey Chapter, National Railway
Historical Society, Inc.; Pages 23, 85, 92, 152, 166, Newark Public Library; Pages
21, 30-35, 40, 42, 46, 78-81, New Jersey Historical Society.

PRINTED IN THE UNITED STATES OF AMERICA

CONTENTS

HISTORY, LEGEND AND NOSTALGIA

Time has forever stilled the hurdy-gurdy lilt of the fabulous merry-go-round. The screams of the roller coaster's riders, the sparkling patter of the Penny Pitch operator, the rumbling of the Dodgem cars and clanking of the Whip are no more. Gone is the sandy white beach beside the cool blue waters of the world's largest outdoor fresh water pool. Captain Joe Basile's brass band is silent, and Bubbles Riccardo at the microphone is a vision growing dim. The roller rink, the beer garden, the funny mirrors, the cotton candy and buttered popcorn are gone forever. Enjoyed by tens of millions during her 79-year reign, Olympic Park has disappeared into history, legend and nostalgia. Yet those fortunate enough to know the way she was will never forget her, and the cherished memories of her days of greatness remain bright.

The history of Olympic Park begins over a century ago, when life was simpler and a summertime outing at a beer garden or country picnic grove was a delightful Sunday tradition.

1

AUF NACH BECKERS WALD!

"A sacred stillness broods over the town," observed a newspaperman who visited Newark one Sunday a decade after the Civil War ended. "No petty shops are open, no horsecars tinkle their bells through the shaded streets. . . . There is even very little private riding or driving in the smoothly graded thoroughfares, so strongly does public opinion set against the practice." Visitors were astonished to find that New Jersey's largest city still observed the Lord's Day with old-fashioned serenity. Despite the presence of tens of thousands of Irish and German immigrants, the rigid traditions of Newark's Puritan founders were very much in evidence.

Less than a mile to the west of Broad and Market Streets, however, Sunday's "sacred stillness" lasted only until the churches emptied. At the stroke of noon, with an enthusiasm that scandalized Newark's first families, the people of Schmerkaese County (as the German district along Springfield Avenue west of Belmont was called) set out to enjoy their day of rest. The truth of that old German proverb—"Eating and drinking holds body and soul together"—was never more evident than on a balmy Sunday afternoon on Springfield Avenue. Wurzburger, Pilsner, Dortmunder and Muenchener flowed from the taps in amber streams. In the beer gardens, or "lager parks," thousands sat at long tables singing the songs of the Fatherland between steins of frothy lager. Crunchy pretzels and salted peanuts competed for space on tables piled high with mouth-watering delicatessen. While children frolicked on a small horse-powered carousel, their elders tapped their feet to the oomp-pah-pah of a brass band or played pinochle at marble-topped tables under the leafy trees.

A score of beer gardens dotted the hill: Vincentz's Park, Erb's Garden and Schlegel's Park had been serving friendly glasses of beer since Civil War days. Beda Voigt's Caledonian Park was the largest of the newer parks, and the most popular. Others were Frank Doelger's Prospect Park, the Newark Schuetzen-Park, Union Park and Saenger Hall Garden, both managed by Voigt, Oscar Seifert's Park, Adolph Hensler's Garden and Weiss' Phoenix Park. Gustav Schmid's Jumbo Brauerei on Hayes Street featured Old Fashioned lager brewed on the premises. While the rest of Newark quietly rocked Sunday away on its front porches, Schmerkaese County joyfully indulged its passion for "Limburger cheese, Sauerkraut, a string of sausages and lager beer."

By law, Newark's 1,300 saloons were officially closed on Sundays, but for many years the police had looked the other way. Gradually pressure mounted to enforce the Sunday laws, gaining momentum in 1877 when prominent clergymen and others formed the Newark Law and Order League, a group dedicated to the proposition that Sunday beer drinking by the city's foreigners was an evil to be suppressed. The League's periodic campaigns to shut down city taverns met stiff opposition from Newark's Germans who from time immemorial had associated Sundays not only with worship but amusement as well.

Traditionally, the season for merry-making began the first week in May. "The weatherman predicted showers, which meant the day would be clear, so the weather was quite favorable for a May excursion to the groves and parks just now assuming their summer garb," wrote the New Jersey *Deutsche Zeitung* in 1887. "The thousands of happy people who went on excursion enjoyed the beautiful spring day, regaining that sense of equilibrium so necessary to good health. Soon the time for singing and dancing will be here and, under the green trees, young and old together will enjoy the pleasures and high spirits of the season." In a city where the enjoyment of a stein of cool lager was reckoned an inalienable right, the do-gooders were doomed to failure.

Efforts by the Law and Order League to stamp out Sunday beer drinking were largely ineffective anyway. The city's relentless westward expansion swallowed up many of the old-time beer gardens. At the same time, improvements in public transportation, especially the extension of the horse car lines, made it easier for fun-seekers to escape beyond the city's limits. "Although the sky was clouded yesterday still hundreds celebrated Pfingst Sunday in the old-fashioned manner," reported the Newark *News* in May 1885. "A number of parties sought the mountains and woods early in the morning, while others waited until afternoon, when they visited the parks. About 500 excursionists and May walkers visited Eagle Rock. . . . Several stages went up filled with shop girls without escorts. . . . The shady roads along the Orange Mountains were traversed by many merry groups of May walkers with their hands filled with flowers." Eagle Rock, with its panoramic view of the metropolitan area, and Hemlock Falls in Millburn, a stunningly beautiful spot, attracted thousands of visitors—and not a few keg-laden brewery wagons as well. Those less inclined to scale the mountain steeps flocked to Becker's Grove, as Olympic Park was first known. Opened in 1887 when the Law and Order League was at its most persistent, the grove rapidly became a favorite with Germans from Newark, Elizabeth and surrounding areas.

"May's first Sunday was up fresh and smiling with spring's brightest sunshine," recorded the *News* in 1889. "Hundreds left the city because of the simple pleasure attending a May walk on such a glorious day, while hundreds of others sought the popular country resorts with the avowed purpose of taking unto themselves or into themselves great quantities of the amber-hued, foam-crowned liquid, dear to the heart of many of the convivially inclined. As a general thing few unpleasant features marred the day, and

scenes of disorder were limited to the parties that started out inordinately provisioned with brewery supplies."

"Becker's 'Amber Mine' is a thickly-wooded grove, bisected by a stream which serves as the boundary line of South Orange and Clinton Townships. The stream bears the rugged name of Big Bear Creek, but many people insist on calling it 'Big Beer Creek.' Over 3,000 merrymakers held high carnival there from dawn to darkness."

"Long before sunrise, hundreds were seen going through Irvington, some riding and a great many on foot. The visitors were principally Germans, and were wending their way to the resort. Mr. [Frank] Buehler, the Springfield Avenue brewer, has leased the grove from Mr. [John] Becker and proposes to make a big summer resort of it. The Maplewood stage was loaded with passengers every trip. . . ."

The grove, continued the *News*, "is about half a mile from the horse cars at Irvington, and contains a dancing pavilion, a bowling alley, a rifle range and on the outside a large ball ground, all of which are well-patronized. The game of ball yesterday was between two picked nines, and as there were several professional players in the field it proved an interesting contest, and resulted in a victory for the Newark players by a score of 8 to 7."

"After the game the players went back to the grove, where they indulged in beer, and in a short time a fight was in progress. . . . It seemed as though everybody was fighting, and several young men from Irvington were roughly handled." As Hilton had no policemen and Irvington's officers lacked jurisdiction, explained the *News*, "the visitors do about as they please."

Two weeks later, the *News* reported that some 5,000 people had visited the grove on Sunday, many arriving at daybreak. The Bayrischer Saengerbund, the National Turnverein, the Friendship Club and Franklin Fire Co. No. 1 held outings at the grove. "Everything went on smoothly until about 2 o'clock," grumbled the paper, "when the beer began to take effect, and all the afternoon young men and boys could be seen lying about the grove in an intoxicated condition. A number of women, some not more than 12 or 14 years of age, were hardly able to stand up." Buehler's arrest on a charge of violating the Sunday law failed to stop the flow of lager, although one unnecessarily mournful young man "was seen walking around with a piece of crepe on his coat." Merrymakers brought their own beer. Those not provisioned with the amber fluid found a ready supply in the dressing room of the Hilton Base Ball Club at three cents a glass.

The *News* was outraged by the "ruffianly actions and shameful orgies" of the Sunday revellers. If the law could be enforced in the city, demanded the paper, why not in the country too? "The conditions which attend the orgies and bacchanalian bouts which take place in the woods and parks beyond the city limits are particularly offensive. . . . The by-lanes and the thoroughfares are infested with brawling fellows and many young women, whose sense of propriety lessens in proportion to the diminution of the chances of detection or exposure to the public gaze. Beer and more fiery fluids are dispensed openly; wagons loaded with beer kegs and men fill the roads in the early hours of the morning."

Proper Newarkers, their Victorian sensibilities offended, found the goings-on at Becker's Grove reprehensible. But the city's Germans feared a dreary Sunday and a dry throat more than the disapproval of their neighbors. Sunday outings to the grove were to remain a fixture of Newark life for more than 15 years.

Olympic Park's story begins with John A. Becker, an affluent member of Newark's German community who bought a small farm on Boyden Avenue in what is now Maplewood from his father-in-law, Alexander Jardin, in December 1868. So captivated were Becker and his wife by the farm's beauty that within a few years they moved from Newark to a new home near Jacoby Street. Becker gradually purchased the surrounding property until he owned a large partially wooded tract that stretched north to Chancellor Avenue.

In 1872, the Mutual Homestead Association acquired 25 acres of prime farmland adjoining Becker's woods to the north, dividing the tract, which ran from Chancellor to Springfield Avenues and from 40th to 45th Streets, into 170 homesites. Members of the association were expected to acquire title to the lots after three or four years of monthly payments. The Mutual Homestead Association was one of several groups organized after the Civil War by Newark's Germans to encourage thrift and enable workingmen to own their own suburban homes. Becker himself was president of the association and one of its chief promoters. Visitors to the Mutual Homestead tract were struck by the tranquil beauty of the majestic woods bordering Chancellor Avenue; many of them, having inspected their lots, crossed the dirt road to spread picnic baskets under the welcome shade of Becker's trees. As the years passed the popularity of Becker's woods increased. Although there was no organized activity of any kind, picnickers rambled through the woods, gathering mushrooms and picking violets. It was a place where a family could enjoy a basket lunch of wurst, a glass of lager and a game or two of horseshoes.

John A. Becker

Becker, who knew most of his visitors personally, decided to make the most of the situation by turning a portion of his woods into an amusement park. A few acres were cleared, a bowling alley, rifle range, swings, dancing pavilion and barroom constructed and on May 8, 1887, Becker's son, William, who would manage the place, announced that the park was open for business: "John Becker's well-known woods has been prepared for the comfort of organizations and families planning May and summer excursions," said the ad in the Newark *Tribüne*, a German newspaper. "Reservations may be made at the site."

Young Becker managed the park during its first two seasons. The saloon, a large one-story frame building, was kept well-stocked with beer and wine. Sausages and cheese were always available and a small string band, an accordianist or several zither players provided the dance music. Pfingstfest, or Whitsuntide, was the first holiday of the spring season. "The honored public is hereby most respectfully informed that Whitsuntide will be celebrated in the most delightful fashion at Becker's Farm," announced young Becker in the *Tribüne* of May 29, 1887. "There will be baseball games morning and afternoon and later, on Springfield Avenue, a spectacular bicycle race. The best of refreshments are at hand, and everyone is welcome." The baseball field, used regularly by the Hilton Base Ball Club, proved especially popular when the Law and Order League managed to halt the flow of lager in the barroom. Baseball without beer was unthinkable, and the convivial players were always willing to sell a few glasses to thirsty spectators. The Irvington-Maplewood-Millburn Memorial Day bicycle race on Springfield Avenue, a major event that drew twenty to thirty thousand spectators, passed within several hundred feet of the park.

Frank Buehler, who owned the German-American Brewing Co. on Springfield Avenue, Newark, and the Germania Hall and beer garden next door, leased the park for the 1889 season. "Auf nach Beckers Wald!," commanded his ad in the *Tribüne*. "Up to Becker's woods!" Wrote Buehler: "The undersigned takes this opportunity to announce to all associations, lodges and clubs that he has taken over the distinguished amusement place in Irvington known as Becker's Woods. Arrangements for excursions and similar functions can be made with him." Buehler's reign was glorious but brief: After his arrest for violating the Sunday law, he was forced to close the saloon, the park's real money-maker. In 1890, his associate,

Louis Ost, took over Becker's Woods. "Fresh eggs, milk, butter, cheese, cigars, beer and all sorts of drinks are always available," advertised Ost. "Vehicles for transportation to the park stand at readiness in Irvington. A genuine German regulation skittle alley as well as a shooting gallery are here for your pleasure." Ost opened the park on weekdays for club outings and on Sundays featured concerts by popular singers.

Although Becker died in 1892, leaving the property to his four grandchildren, the park continued as before. In 1893, Gertrude Zimmer leased it for the season, advertising its attractions in *Der Erzähler*, the Sunday edition of the New Jersey *Freie Zeitung:* "To clubs and societies as well as all who wish to spend a delightful day, I recommend Becker's well-known woods. A shooting gallery, nine-pin skittle alley and swing stand at your command. Good food and drink, fresh eggs, milk and all kinds of cheese are always available." Mrs. Zimmer added a kitchen where warm meals could be prepared. Sunday concerts remained a regular feature and picnickers were always welcome.

Like their countrymen elsewhere in America, Newark's Germans organized themselves into innumerable singing societies, pleasure clubs, lodges and Turnverein. There was a club for every purpose, ranging from the Independent Germania Rifle Association and the German Veteran's Society of the

Members of the Aurora Singing Society of Newark on an outing at Becker's Woods, June 3, 1889.

Newark tavern owner Hans Hartwig (third from right, top row) *managed the grove in 1897 and 1898.*

Franco-Prussian War to the Merry Circle Bowling Club, the Century Skat Club and the Gottfried Krueger Guard, plus more than a score of Saengerbund. Nearly all of them held outings at Becker's Woods. The singing societies in particular gathered regularly at the park, especially when Buehler, who was treasurer of the Bayrischer Saengerbund, managed the place. The shooting gallery attracted the rifle clubs, the baseball field and bicycle track, added at mid-decade, drew the Turnverein, and the skittle alley, the bowling clubs.

In 1897, Frank Buehler, Louis Schultz and Gustave A. Grub signed a long-term lease with the Becker heirs. Hans Hartwig, a Newark tavern owner who managed the grove in 1897 and 1898, boasted in his advertising that Hilton Park, as it was now called, was "the coolest and shadiest amusement park in Essex County." When Buehler resumed active management of Hilton Park in 1899, he added a second ball field and bowling alley, installed electric lights and enlarged the restaurant. The Irvington and Hilton trolley now stopped directly in front of the park's gate after a nickel ride from downtown Newark. Sacred concerts were scheduled on Sundays, while strolling musicians entertained the crowds afternoons and evenings. Dancers crowded the open-air pavilion nightly.

The park's musical offerings were remarkably varied, a tradition that would last for more than half a century. During the second week of June, 1902, for example, Buehler featured Helen May Butler and her Ladies' Military Band. "This organization will give concerts there every afternoon and evening," said the *News*, "and from accounts of its performances elsewhere much enjoyment may be anticipated by patrons. . . . Miss Butler directs the only military band in this country composed wholly of women." A month later, Voss' First Regiment Band was featured with Joe Tannenbaum singing favorite scenes from German opera.

Unlike several other small amusement parks in Essex County, Hilton Park had no mechanical rides, but they would have been out of place. The magnificent trees and grassy violet-strewn fields, the soothing music of the zither, guitar and mandolin, mouth-watering delicatessen, aromatic cigars and cool, foamy steins of lager beer, the Schuetzenfest and Saengerfest—these were what the crowds who flocked there during the spring and summer months came for. Buehler proclaimed Hilton Park "the most beautiful recreation grounds in the state." His satisfied patrons agreed: 'Ja, alles ist gemütlich hier!"

2

A NEW PLACE
OF ENJOYMENT

Americans who came of age at the turn of the century had little patience for the genteel Victorian ways of their parents. The urban middle class was especially eager for amusements more irreverent and less inhibited than the Sunday afternoon excursions so popular in the 19th century. After Coney Island caught the public's fancy in the late 1890s, a craze for outdoor amusements swept the nation. Within a matter of years every city of any size had an amusement park, and the larger ones boasted four or five. Increased leisure time, fatter paychecks and inexpensive rapid public transportation made the amusement park possible. By 1919 there were over 1,500 parks in the country, so many in fact that, as one writer put it, it was "almost possible to ride from the East Coast to the West Coast on roller coasters."

Newark saw three amusement parks open within the space of as many years. Electric Park on South Orange Avenue, which opened for business on Memorial Day, 1903, was the first. Located on the site of the old Schuetzen Park, Electric Park featured vaudeville performances in a rustic open-air theatre, a dancing pavilion, merry-go-round, toboggan slide, a menagerie, an Old Mill ride and a novel electric fountain that gave the place its name. "It is an artistic spectacle," raved the Newark *News* of the fountain, "combining classic posings and tableaux in which handsome young women suitably attired and surrounded by hundreds of electric lights appear, while the water shoots upward for a hundred feet." Two years later

another park opened on the Nutley-Belleville border. Hillside Pleasure Park offered a dancing pavilion, mechanical rides and a permanent Wild West Show complete with Indians, Rough Riders and real shoot 'em up cowboys.

Both Electric Park and Hillside Pleasure Park were short-lived. Electric Park, later the site of the Newark Motordrome, closed its gates in 1912 after a spectacular motorcycle accident killed eight and injured nearly a score. Hillside Pleasure Park, its name changed to Riviera Park, went into receivership in 1927 after "too many rainy Sundays."

Most successful of Newark's three amusement parks was Olympic Park, which opened on May 28, 1904, for a glorious, never-to-be forgotten reign that would last more than 61 years. A blizzard of extravagant publicity heralded Olympic's debut: "Those who have not visited the park this season will be astonished at the transformation," marvelled the Newark *Daily Advertiser* on opening day. "Progress is being made with the arena, which is being constructed for aerial acts, and the finishing touches are being given the funniest of all pleasure resort attractions, the 'helter-skelter.' The underbush, stones, stumps and other obstructions have been carefully cleared away, and the hollows have been filled in. . . . Space on the old baseball lot has been given to the management of a circus, which has been booked for an indefinite period, and every available bit of room will be taken up by attractions. . . ."

The main gate with its classical theme, from a postcard, c. 1906.

The *Freie Zeitung,* New Jersey's leading German language paper, called Olympic Park "a new place of enjoyment" for German families. "What used to be Hilton Park, better known as Becker's Woods, will open today and tomorrow as Olympic Park. The new owners have made Becker's Woods a first class amusement park. An outstanding group of musicians, Victor's Royal Venetian Band, who had a sensational following in New York City in previous summers, will furnish popular and classical music every day of the week from 2 P.M. to 11 P.M. On the newly-built arena astonishing circus acts will perform, including Japanese trapeze artists, European balancers, three trained dogs, talking geese, and so forth. There are hundreds of additional amusements in the park. The Helter-Skelter, an exact copy of the one at Luna Park, Coney Island, will provide very special entertainment. No extra admission will be charged for all these amusements. Two camels may be ridden in the park by both young and old. A miniature railroad, consisting of a locomotive and 10 cars, will transport patrons around the park. The entire establishment is like a fairy land, lighted with thousands of electric lights. . . . A colossal dance hall is being constructed 150 feet long and 80 feet wide. That the kitchen and cellar will offer the best in food and drink is guaranteed by the renown of the Colosseum."

"When the gates of the new Olympic Park are thrown open to the public next Saturday," enthused the Newark *Sunday News,* "local pleasure seekers will have reasons to congratulate themselves upon this addition to the number of nearby outing resorts. As a place for recreation and amusement it promises to rank among the most attractive of its kind in this section. Finely wooded and naturally attractive, the place is being transformed by a lavish expenditure of money on the part of the new management and by the ingenuity of skilled artisans and landscape gardeners into an enticing spot."

"A new and imposing entrance, a feature of which is four huge pillars, entwined with electric lights, has been constructed, and descending from the arch over the main gateway will be the word, 'Olympic,' in letters of fire. Electricity will play an important part in the decorative scheme of the grounds, as over 2,000 vari-colored incandescent lamps will be used to lighten up the dense foliage of the trees at night and to give a spectacular appearance to the scene. In the immediate rear of the entrance have been placed two statues, representing lions, and copied from masterpieces in the Champs Elysee, in Paris. Each is 13 feet in height, and, being finished in gilt, is a very noticeable object. The old dining pavilion is being converted into an exhibition hall that will contain picture ma-

Lower end of the grove. The sign on the ice cream stand reads, "Original Famous Cones Filled with Ice Cream."

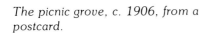

The picnic grove, c. 1906, from a postcard.

The Promenade ran from the main gate to the opera house.

chines, phonographic and other amusing devices. A Midway, supplied with a shooting gallery, merry-go-round, swings, gypsy fortune-tellers and go-carts and ponies, will be an attractive feature of the place. A women's parlor, in the form of an ancient castle, has been erected, and a larger and more modern band pavilion replaces the old one."

"The men who have become proprietors of the Olympic and whose money is working such a transformation in the resort are Christian Kurz, and his brother-in-law, Herman Schmidt," added the *Sunday News*. "The arrangements made by them to preserve order, even when the park may be most crowded, are such that women and children are assured protection from any kind of annoyance."

Schmidt, a 44-year-old Newark businessman, and Kurz, who owned the Colosseum, a popular Springfield Avenue restaurant and beer garden, were inspired by the overnight success of Electric Park to try the same formula at Hilton Park. They poured some $20,000 into the venture, named the park in honor of the Olympic Games held that year in St. Louis and opened on Memorial Day weekend to a gratifyingly large crowd. Schmidt and Kurz took the scenic beauty

Gilt lions stand guard behind the main gate, from a postcard.

of Becker's Woods, added amusements, vaudeville, a circus, dancing pavilion and fine restaurant to create a park that was successful from the start.

"Its many natural advantages combine with an attractive entertainment bill to make Olympic Park one of the most popular family resorts in the vicinity of the city," reported the *Daily Advertiser* a week after the park opened. "Within easy reach at the cost of a five-cent trolley fare of the various residence sections as well as of the business centres of Newark, not the smallest of the attractions offered by a visit to the new park is the delightful ride through pleasant scenery."

"When the park is reached, too, the eye is gratified by resting on a beautiful natural grove in the midst of which the management has arranged its attractions. Comfortable benches with tables to match are placed at short intervals all over the park, beneath the shade of the trees, so that family groups may refresh themselves with something more substantial than ozone, while they are watching one or other of the many 'still turns' provided for their entertainment on the great square stage in the centre of the grounds. These include acts by the Yamamoto brothers, wire walkers and balancers; James Irwin, in a trapeze balancing specialty; the Mohrens, also trapeze artists; Kenyon and De Garmo, gymnasts and balancers; Sam Balmon, in a novelty act; Raymond, the 'human pin-wheel;' and others. . . ."

"Mindful of the popularity usually attached to a 'Midway' feature, the management has provided a Moorish palace, an exploration of whose mysteries will well repay the curious. Nor have the little ones been forgotten. In addition to camel riding and other sports not indigenous to the soil of New Jersey, what is called a 'Helter-Skelter' has been erected, which has already become one of the most popular features in the park. The 'Helter-Skelter' is a spiral slide or toboggan, to the summit of which the youngsters ascend

Leon and Adeline, 1904

The Helter-Skelter or Human Toboggan, from a postcard printed in Leipzig, Germany.

by a guarded stairway reaching about 20 feet in the air. Then squatting at the top of the slide, off they go and down and around they are whirled until in a couple of seconds they are landed safely on a soft platform at the foot, having enjoyed all the delightful sensations of shooting the chutes or sliding down a cellar door. A couple of women attendants are present to care for the smaller children, so that their mothers may enjoy the other entertainments without worrying about their young one's safety."

"Children of a larger growth who delight in dancing will be given an opportunity of tripping it on the light fantastic too. Work is being pushed on the erection of a big dance pavilion which will soon be ready for the enjoyment of the spielers. Altogether the management has made a good start and if present indications are a guide, they will succeed in their declared aim of providing an ideal family resort."

Wholesome fun for the entire family was the proclaimed goal of the park's new owners. Schmidt, Kurz and their general manager, Hans Wevers, never

sought to recreate Coney Island in New Jersey. Instead, their park was a delightful blend of tranquility and excitement, of picnic grove and vaudeville show, of beer garden and circus. To be sure, there were mechanical rides for patrons who demanded that sort of thing, but there were never more than three or four. Billed in the early days as "The Eldorado of Essex County," Olympic Park was far tamer than the ads suggested. Emphasis was on the family and attractions that would appeal to every age group. The dance pavilion and restaurant were first-class, the circus, menagerie and vaudeville shows the equal of those at any summer resort in the state. The Midway offered a variety of attractions but it was small by the standards of the day.

Food and drink were in abundant supply. Picnic tables scattered under the trees could accommodate 2,500 at a time. Although many patrons brought their own picnic baskets, those who did not could buy cheese, frankfurters, homemade potato salad, cole slaw, sausages and the specialty of the park, thick

ABOVE — *A 1905 automobile outing.* BELOW — *The main gate was fully illuminated at night. The tavern is to the right. Circa 1907.*

slices of German rye bread spread lavishly with cottage cheese or sour cream. Beer, wine and soda were available at the tavern.

If the cuisine smacked of Germany, the local transportation did not. Matsuma Ben Rahmin, "a native Arabian," offered a whiff of the Mideast as he guided patrons around the park on his camels and elephants.

Spectacular circus acts were Wevers' forte, and the 1904 season was typical. Park patrons watched spellbound as Blondin, the Human Torch, jumped enveloped in flames from a platform 75 feet in the air into a four-foot-deep tank of water. They cheered when Professor Alfreno, the High Wire King, performing at tree-top level, ignited the fireworks attached to his costume. In fact, fireworks were to be one of Olympic Park's trademarks. On weekends, the evening circus performance closed with a thunderous display of rockets, pinwheels and sparklers. Ground-level pyrotechnics were artistic wonders, including the burning of Rome by Nero, the battle of Gettysburg and "The Sensational Spectacle of Niagara Falls."

Schmidt and Kurz advertised the park heavily in Newark's English and German language press, attracting huge crowds throughout the summer of 1904. A trio of front-page stories helped draw the curious. In August, Cleo and Nero, two of the lions on display in the menagerie, nearly took off the hand of their trainer, Herr Roberti. That same week an 18-year-old high diver broke his back during a performance. And a month later, Sultan the lion fatally mauled a careless patron who reached into the cage to stroke his fur.

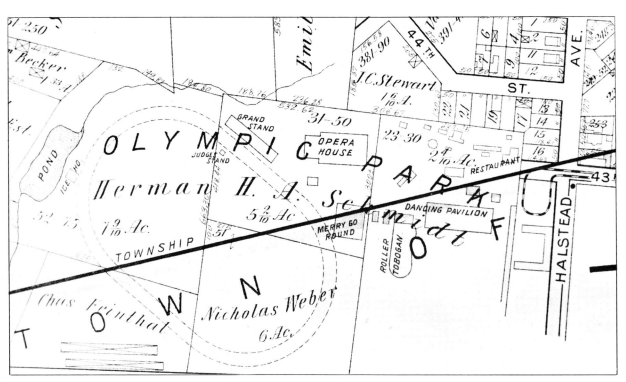

From a 1906 map of Irvington and Maplewood.

3

OCEANS OF BEER

No sooner did the gates close on Olympic Park's 1904 season than Schmidt and Kurz began planning an extensive and costly renovation of the park. Throughout the early months of 1905, crews supervised by Manager Wevers laid water and drainage pipes, installed utility lines and covered the paths and roads with cinders. A new ballroom, theatre and restaurant were built at a cost of $45,000. Another $11,500 went for electric lighting and landscaping. When the park's second season began on May 27, the "pleasure resort," as the papers called it, had been transformed. Said the Newark News: "Always a delightful retreat in the summer time because of its shady groves and agreeable woodland character, the many improvements introduced by those now in control have greatly increased its charms for those seeking recreation and amusement."

Among the most notable improvements, added the News, was the theatre, which could seat 2,500, a new two story dining pavilion with 400 tables for both a la carte and table d'hote service, "an immense electric merry-go-round," a roller coaster, shooting gallery, a well-stocked menagerie and a sanded playground for children. "The park will be particularly attractive at night, owing to the brilliant and picturesque lighting of the grounds by thousands of incandescent lamps. Every evening a pyrotechnic display including pieces representing prominent persons, will be a feature of the entertainment. Not the least of the attractions will be the dancing pavilion, which was so largely patronized last season, and in which Benzler's fine band will furnish music for those wishing to enjoy dancing on the smooth and ample floor."

The 1905 season opened with record-breaking crowds that continued straight through Labor Day. The new rides, the fireworks displays and the garlands of electric lights strung throughout the grove evoked the expected oohs and ahs. Featuring "reasonable prices. . .and well-prepared and wholesome food," the dining pavilion proved especially popular. The table d'hote menu for the Memorial Day weekend was a mouth-watering melange of American, German and French dishes:

MENU

Pickles, Olives, Radishes
Consomme
Potage a la Windsor

Turbot Puree au Chablis
Potatoes Parisienne

Pate de Kolnille a la Reine

Leg of Lamb   Braise a la Chabeur
Green Peas   Leipziger Medley

Roast Philadelphia Capon
Prime Ribs of Beef au jus
Compote   Salad

Royal Pudding au Caramel

Christian Kurz

As an added attraction, the table d'hote menu was priced at 50 cents from noon to 3p.m. daily.

Equally popular were the afternoon and evening vaudeville performances given in the theatre. The opening week bill was typical of the park's offerings that year: comedians Ascott and Eddie appearing in a sketch called "Things That Happen;" "Chalk" Saunders, the crayon artist and comedian whose specialty was "Physogs;" Ezier and Webb, comedians; Harry La Rose and Co. in "a laughter-provoking skit" entitled, "The Sailor and the Horse;" Winchermann's acrobatic bears and monkeys; Johnson and Wells, "the colored comedians who have the reputation of being fashion plates in comedy;" and Leo Dervalto, "who mounts on a revolving globe to the top of a spiral incline, 33 feet in height." In the weeks that followed, comedians, banjoists, acrobats, dog acts, colored entertainers, shadow and ragtime dancers, diving horses, trained pigs, magicians, singers, monkeys and jugglers entertained the crowds with performances one newspaper called "the best that are to be seen in

Feldmann's trained high-diving pigs, July 1905. The park's new roller coaster (called a roller toboggan in those days) *is at the far right.*

ABOVE — *The restaurant, and* BELOW — *The dancing pavilion, both from a 1909 brochure. "The management," said the brochure, "has always striven to maintain a high class family rendezvous. . . . We want to assure you that if you come here you need have no fear of contamination with the undesirable element usually found at summer amusement resorts."*

the better class of summer resorts." A series of short motion pictures closed each show.

Not the least of the park's attractions was the grove. "Covering a large section of the grounds, it is one of the finest in this neighborhood, and its natural beauty has been enhanced by the work of the landscape gardener," reported a Newark paper. "As the park is located on high ground, away from the smoke and the dust of the city, its atmosphere is pure and envigorating, and this fact is not the least of its charms for those who cannot get away to mountains or seashore in hot weather, but can find pleasant shade and cooling breezes in this nearby and easily accessible resort."

Olympic Park's popularity with Newark's German-Americans led to its selection as the site of the 21st National Saengerfest of the North-Eastern Saengerbund of America, held July 1-4, 1906. An association of German singing societies from New York, New Jersey, Pennsylvania, Maryland, Delaware and the District of Columbia, the Saengerbund convened every three years to celebrate "the charm of German music and song." Saengerfest programs included German folksongs and Heimatlieder as well as the more serious music of the immortal German and Austrian composers. Competition among the choristers was intense and the enthusiasm of both singers and audiences was enormous.

Schmidt began preparing for the event early in 1905, spending thousands on a wooden concert hall measuring 90 by 160 feet and scores of canvas tents to serve as headquarters for the many singing societies expected to attend. An additional trolley spur laid from Springfield Avenue was finished in the nick of time. The 1906 festival, the second held in the Newark area, drew some 5,000 singers representing more than a hundred organizations in 40 cities. Chartered trains brought a thousand visitors from Philadelphia, another 700 from Baltimore. Hundreds more journeyed from points as distant as Wilmington, Del., and Lancaster, Pa.

The four-day festival opened with a gala concert at the park on July 1. Five thousand people crowded into Schmidt's new hall, more than half of them forced to stand in the aisles or along the walls, as the New York Philharmonic under the baton of Julius Lorenz, the festival's music director, launched what the Newark *News* called "the great festival of harmony." The stirring chords of Wagner's "Tannhauser" overture and a "Hymn of Welcome," especially written for the occasion and sung by a male chorus of 560, set the tone for one of the largest events ever held at Olympic Park. An estimated 25,000 people jammed the grounds daily before the festival closed on the Fourth of July with the contest for the blue ribbon of German choral singing, the coveted Kaiser Prize.

According to a newsman who was there, the thousands who took cars daily to Olympic Park to enjoy the music lost precious few opportunities to satisfy the inner man as well. "The merry-go-rounds, the ring and stick men, and the picture post-card sellers had more than they could do," reported the New York *Times* of opening day. "Then there was the 'Twirly-

A front-page Newark Evening News *photo of conductor Julius Lorenz leading the New York Philharmonic Orchestra in the opening concert, July 1, 1906.*

One of the singing societies at the 21st National Saengerfest competing for the $20,000 trophy offered by Kaiser Wilhelm II. From Harper's Weekly.

Whirly' for the children, and the crowds of little ones found how easy it is to go downhill sitting down in a smooth and curly shoot. Some of their elders went in, of course, only to hold the baby, and there were the most fascinating collisions at the end, when some little girl would not get out of the way fast enough and others piled up on top of her."

"But these amusements may be seen any day at Coney Island, and there was something far more characteristic of a Saengerfest than that. Near the entrance to the park were scores of long tables, and an open-air van hard by. Dozens of people sat on the rough benches under the shady trees and emptied steins all the afternoon and evening. At the other end of the grounds a veritable camp had been erected, and to every singing society was assigned a tent, a long table, and a row of empty steins. To fill these, two large depots had been erected where casks innumerable of lager were kept stored on ice. From these a continuous procession of men took barrels to the tents, and soon each verein was holding open house to all who came along. With it all the crowd was most orderly and the police had nothing to do but look after strayed children. As the evening drew on, the Saengerfest became a singing festival indeed. Clubs drew together and stood in groups and sang the glees of the Fatherland. The women joined in, too, and as the twilight fell, from all parts of the camp might be heard rounds and catches sung in proper time and tune."

After the Kaiser Prize was awarded and the festival officially closed, said the Newark *News*, the "scenes at the park. . .were such as to be long retained in the memory. It was then the carnival spirit became riotous, though decently so. The fun that began earlier in the day and found vent in antics, impromptu concerts and fraternal visits, with frequent toasting in the popular German beverage, was cut loose from all restrictions as the last hours came. Men and women, too, formed in lines at the tents and, following their several organization banners, marched up and down the streets of the 'city of tents,' saluting and serenading their fraternal brethren. Strains of music and song poured forth on every side, and oceans of beer were consumed."

TOP — *An overflow crowd listening to the concert through the open windows.* MIDDLE — *Singers on their way to Saengerfest Hall.* BOTTOM — *The entrance to the hall. Both the Newark* Evening News *and New York* Times *covered the Saengerfest extensively.*

4

THE CLASSIEST RESORT IN AMERICA

In April 1909, *Billboard*, the magazine of the entertainment industry, called Olympic Park "one of the finest, shadiest and most accommodating parks in the East, easy to reach by trolley." With an average daily attendance of 10,000, continued the publication, the park "is growing so rapidly that [Herman Schmidt] is always ready to add further developments, and he expects to have a little city of his own in a few years, by which time he hopes to reach the top notch and will continue to improve the enterprise until the business shows an income of a half million dollars a season."

Schmidt had good reason to be optimistic as the park's sixth season began. In a few short years, Olympic had become the clear favorite of Essex County pleasure seekers, far outdistancing Electric Park and Hillside Pleasure Park in popularity, thanks to Schmidt's keen talent for attracting and keeping his customers. The park was always clean and the crowds orderly. The opera house and dining and dancing pavilion drew what the press called "a better class" of patrons, while the picnic grove and Midway appealed broadly to family groups and the young. Sports fanciers flocked to the racetrack. Constant renovation of the park's features cost thousands, but the investment paid off handsomely in steadily increasing attendance. Acutely sensitive to changes in public taste, Schmidt hunted far and wide for crowd-pullers, signing many of the best entertainers of the era.

Free afternoon and evening vaudeville on the open-air stage was an Olympic Park tradition. Every year, a seemingly inexhaustible procession of jugglers, acrobats, singers, comedians, strongmen, dancers, aerialists, trained dogs, pigs, monkeys, horses and mules crossed the stage, booked through the Keith-Proctor circuit and later the Frank A. Keeney organization in New York City. Each show consisted of eight to 12 acts and lasted about 60 minutes, which was about the limit spectators were willing to stand. Seats were provided only during the few weeks before and after the opera season when performances were shifted to the theatre. During Schmidt's 12 years, some 1,000 acts appeared at the park. The variety was mind-boggling: Kit Karsen, in a novel shooting act; the Carmen Sisters, expert banjoists; Doherty's dog circus, featuring 15 snow white poodles; the Randolphs, grotesque acrobats; Ah Ling Foo, a Chinese illusionist; May Clinton, the world-famous sharpshooter; Tom Bateman, the dancing sailor; Burnette and Marcella, comic acrobats; the Balfour Trio, trapeze artists; The Great Inman, a European contortionist; and, in 1915, Mae West, billed as "one of the best comediennes now on the vaudeville stage."

Two of 1906's finest acts were German's high diving horses, a pair of milk-white Arabian steeds named King and Queen trained to dive 30 feet into a pool of water, and Mlle. Loubet, a daring young lady who coasted down a long runway in an "auto-truck," gaining speed before making a flying loop across a

ABOVE — *The park's new entrance, strikingly similar to the Brandenburg Gate in Berlin.* BELOW — *The Administration Building. Both are from postcards, c.1909, a time when Olympic was billed as "New Jersey's Foremost Pleasure Resort."*

ABOVE — *Olympic's original Merry-Go-Round looked out on one of the park's many beautiful gardens.* BELOW — *Foreground, from left to right, the Ice Cream Stand, entrance to the Roller Coaster, Rifle Range, Photo Stand and Merry-Go-Round.*

16-foot chasm. Among headliners in later years were Big Jeff, a trained kangaroo skilled in the art of boxing; Hayco, the Handcuff King, whose act included "an attempt to extricate himself from a steel-bound packing case which has been securely closed by a committee of carpenters;" and Oklahoma's Miss Olive Swan and her educated Spanish mules. Miss Swan's mules were a highlight of the 1911 season, reported the papers: "A particularly strenuous animal named 'Theodore Roosevelt' delights his admirers by displaying a row of pearly teeth with all the pride of his illustrious namesake, while 'Tom Greene' demonstrated the 'soul kiss' with all the intensity of his human competitors." Another favorite was William

Herman H. A. Schmidt

DeWolf Hopper, the noted actor and comedian, who always closed his act with his immortal recitation of "Casey at the Bat." Typically, the evening vaudeville shows ended with what the ads called, "the latest releases in American photoplays," about 10 minutes of newsreels and comedy shorts, and a spectacular fireworks display.

Besides the free vaudeville, the park's major attractions were a large electric merry-go-round run by Fred Dohl, the menagerie, the Helter-Skelter, circle swings, a roller skating rink that opened in 1907, the grove, opera house, roller coaster, two-story restaurant, three-lane bowling alley, racetrack, athletic field, dance pavilion and scenic railway. The sanded playground and pony and donkey rides were re-

served exclusively for the children. The park's grounds were Schmidt's pride and joy. Supervised by Ignatz Mueller, an experienced landscaper, the grounds alone were worth the 10 cent admission charge.

Magnificent flowerbeds featured blooms grown in the park's own greenhouses; each spring some 25,000 plants were set out. In 1908 a huge electric fountain was installed just inside the main gate at the center of the park's major floral display.

"The Classiest Family Resort in America" was more than just an adman's dream. Entry requirements for Olympic Park were always strict. Only gentlemen with coat and tie could be admitted. Even youngsters were expected to wear their Sunday best. Thomas Edison, who lived in West Orange, was among those impressed by the tone of the park: "I never worry when my family visits the park," he wrote to Schmidt, "for I know they are in good hands." The 400-table restaurant was one of the area's finest, offering full course dinners from 25 to 75 cents. Seafood was a specialty and many were the visitors from Newark, Jersey City and New York who arrived by carriage or auto for an evening of fine food and dancing. Whenever opera was in season, the restaurant featured cabaret entertainment. Numerous clubs and associations held their banquets at the restaurant, supping on lobster, plank steak and champagne. "The restaurant, with its seating capacity of 1,500, is a prominent feature of the park," said the Newark *News* in 1911. "White waiters only are employed and the table d'hote and a la carte menus commend them to fastidious tastes. Here are prepared formal dinners, clambakes and special refreshments for automobile parties, clubs, fraternal, church and other societies desiring luncheons, dinners or suppers." The waiters, German-born to a man, wore white shirts and black bow ties.

Music was an ever-present companion of park visitors. In addition to the Aborn Opera Co., Schmidt delighted in booking concert bands as often as possible. John Philip Sousa and Arthur Pryor, world-famous bandleaders, entertained at the park. Benzler's Dance Band and Quintano's Famous Royal Venetian Band played in the dance pavilion. Schmidt's nephew, Herbert Baudistel, led the nine-piece Olympic Park Concert Orchestra beginning in 1911. When the German steamers were interned at Hoboken in 1915, their combined bands gave daily concerts in the opera house. The 30-man Associated Marine Bands played everything from American ragtime to German marches and the classics of the old masters. Some 15,000 listeners heard them during July and August.

To keep his patrons returning year after year, Schmidt staged marathon races, dog shows, aviation meets, an agricultural fair, horse races, automobile and motorcycle races and "athletic carnivals." In May 1910, Schmidt ran a miniature Olympiad complete with a hammer and discus throwing contest, foot races, pole vaulting and hurdle races. A few months later the Olympic Park Athletic Club organized to promote boxing matches at the park. When the 1911 season opened, patrons could enjoy a new athletic field prepared especially for races, baseball games, tournaments and aviation meets.

Public fascination with human flight prompted Schmidt to feature aerial entertainment every year, beginning in 1907. Professor Archie Griffin, the balloonist, awed the crowds that season with "a daring attempt to shake hands with the sun." According to the publicity, Griffin planned to ascend 18,000 feet into the air above Olympic Park before parachuting to earth. In July 1907, Griffin, whose ascents were considerably less than 18,000 feet, was joined by the Wolverine Flier, a dirigible built in the mid-West. "To meet the growing demand for sensational outdoor entertainment, the management has closed a contract. . .for daily exhibitions and flights of the airship, the Wolverine Flier, during the remainder of the season," reported the Newark *News*. "The airship. . .is said to represent the acme of skill and daring in aerial navigation. The Wolverine Flier's first flight from Olympic Park will take place tomorrow afternoon, and after sailing over the park for a short time it will descend to the ground. Its navigator, Ernest Hogan, also will engage in an aerial race with Balloonist Archie Griffin. . . . Besides these special attractions the airship will be on exhibition daily and will make trips to Newark every afternoon delivering messages here." According to the paper, the Wolverine Flier, powered by a "motor-boat type engine," was similar in construction "to the dirigible war balloons and airships now utilized by the military authorities in France and Germany. It resembles a monster bird. . . ."

Several years after the Wolverine Flier made its appearance, one of the largest airships ever seen in the East, a 90-foot dirigible operated by Edward R. Boland and Freddie Owens, putted through the air over Olympic Park. Formerly associated with the aviation meets at Belmont Park, Boland made his tory on August 7, 1911, when he jumped from the dirigible wearing a pioneer version of the manually-operated parachute. In 1911, George Nealy and A.B. Stone exhibited their aeroplanes, taking off daily from the athletic field. During the 1914 and 1915 seasons, Professor Johnny Mack, "the champion aeronaut of the world," and his assistant, Eddie Phillips, repeated Griffin's popular balloon ascension and parachute drop. The first air transportation between Newark and its suburbs dates to September 1911 when young Freddie Owens carried a passenger from Olympic Park to downtown Newark in his Curtiss dirigible. Prudently, both Owens and his passenger strapped on parachutes before takeoff.

Typical of Schmidt's flair for showmanship was his revival of the old Essex County Fair, an annual event for many years at Newark's Waverly Fairgrounds until discontinued at the turn of the century. Schmidt staged his first Agricultural and Industrial Exposition in September 1907. The 10-day event, attended by some 50,000 patrons, featured an art exhibit, floral displays, a poultry, cattle and produce exhibit, dog show, Wild West Show, basketball tournament, automobile parade and races, track and field events, harness races on the oval track, a fireworks display, balloon ascension and the usual throng of politicians eager to mingle among the large crowd of voters.

S. Kikuda, a Japanese juggling act, 1908.

Although the governor failed to attend as promised, reported the Newark *News*, "practically all the county and municipal officials were there. . .and the candidates who hope to succeed them. . . ." Added the paper, with a touch of sarcasm: "The hot sausage man, who produces his goods, except the mustard and rolls, right on the grounds, was more of an attraction to the politicians than the several exhibits of vegetables, fruit, poultry, live stock and manufactured articles." Successive county fairs held in 1908 and 1909 were no less extravagant. In October 1910, the New Jersey State Fair was staged in the park, a six-day event that was the largest ever held in north Jersey. The fair opened on Monday with Military Day, featuring National Guard regiments in exhibits

SEASON
1909

New Jersey's Famous
Summer Entertainment Resort

Swept by Coolest Breezes

GREETINGS FROM

Olympic Park
Newark, N. J.

A Resort That Need Not be Ashamed of Its Reputation

THE Foremost Open-air Resort of New Jersey is a title that has come unsolicited to Olympic Park of Newark. This resort draws from a territory populated by over a million of people, nearly all of whom can reach its gates on a single five-cent fare. ¶ The cut which appears above gives a glimpse of that section of the park which greets the eye as the visitor enters through the arched gateway. In the foreground is the fountain, one of the park's attractive sculptural features, and slightly to the left of it, seen dimly through the trees, the large dance hall

From a 1909 brochure.

An Ideal Location

DELIGHTFULLY situated in a wooded region and on an elevation which affords coolness in the heated season, and the purest of air, this popular centre of entertainment enjoys peculiar advantages that few other similar resorts in this section of the country can claim.

A Glimmer of the Poetic

PRETTY, winding walks and driveways, mottled with the quivering shade of foliage; dainty, lawn-like stretches of greensward curving and spreading in fantastic shapes among the tall tree trunks; shapely beds of blossoms that brighten the sombre places, smile a merry greeting to the sunlight and toss their perfume to the summer air; waters leaping from their cool basin to flash in rainbows and fall in tiny drops of music like the sound of fairy bells. Who would not desert the sweltering, dust-choked city for such delights as these?

Easy of Access by Trolley

IT is the easiest thing in the world to reach Olympic Park by trolley. A double-track loop, especially constructed for the convenience of the patrons of the resort, brings the visitor right to the main entrance. Cars run direct from all points on Newark's two principal thoroughfares—Market and Broad Streets. Take either the " Broad " or " Springfield " line, or transfer to them. ¶ There is no more enjoyable brief trolley trip from the city than down Broad Street with its stately elms and none less stately dwellings; past South and Lincoln Parks; up aristocratic Clinton Avenue, and out through the marvellously growing residential district along Springfield Avenue near the Park.

¶ Olympic Park has also ideal facilities for out-of-town patronage, as trolley cars run to it direct from the principal stations of all the five railroads which enter Newark—the Pennsylvania, Central, Lackawanna, Lehigh Valley and Erie. ¶ It is a favorite objective point for trolley parties from outlying towns and cities. Tally-hos and other carriages likewise bring accessions of merrymakers to swell the outing crowds.

¶ What good is a place if you can't get to it? But everybody can get to Olympic Park.

THEY COME IN TALLY-HOS FOR AN OUTING IN THE PARK

SCENE FROM THE OPEN-AIR VAUDEVILLE

From a 1909 brochure.

31

Olympic Park's Model Restaurant

SOME years ago, a chap got himself more or less famous by claiming to have discovered that the word restaurant was derived from the plural of the Latin word "res," meaning "things," and "taurus," meaning "bull"—bully things. That chap was mistaken, for at the time the English word was invented they didn't know what a good restaurant was, let alone a "bully" one. If they could have enjoyed a visit to a restaurant with a thoroughly up-to-date twentieth century culinary equipment—such as Olympic Park's, for instance—they would have had some justification for springing the pun and the new word at the same time.

¶ In one respect, the restaurant at Olympic Park differs from other up-to-date twentieth century establishments of its sort: it is wide open to the cooling breezes.

¶ Being essentially a summer restaurant, it caters specifically to the summer trade. It takes for granted that its patrons want to keep as cool as possible and to be served with such dishes as will be most pleasing to the palate during the heated term. But, nevertheless, it offers the widest variety of choice. ¶ It makes a specialty of refreshing beverages of all sorts. ¶ In this conveniently situated prandial emporium, 1,500 can be comfortably seated at the same time. Extensive improvements have been made since last season, and here, as elsewhere throughout the Park, visitors will find new and attractive features and better conveniences.

¶ The Restaurant this season will be under the management of one of the most competent Caterers in the Metropolitan District. If by any chance you don't happen to know what's good to eat, he does. ¶ No, gentle reader, these gentlemen are not Turbaned Turks or Afghans. They are the Little Regiment under the command of Olympic Park's Chef.

Comic Opera—Olympic's Stellar Indoor Feature

THE Aborn Opera Company, famous for its past performances at Olympic Park, will appear again this season, afternoon and evening, week days and Sundays, in high-class light and comic operas, at popular prices. A picture of this talented organization is shown on the following page.

¶ No Summer Park Theatre in America has a finer class of audiences than the Olympic Park Opera House. If there is any doubt as to the popularity of the entertainment, glance at the illustration on the page opposite.

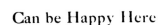

SHEDS FOR AUTOMOBILES AND CARRIAGES

Can be Happy Here

AUTOISTS find Olympic Park ideal for an afternoon, evening or Sunday outing. Sheds and other special conveniences are provided. Essex County has the finest roads in the world, and

All Roads Lead to Olympic Park.

¶ For the women and children there are a thousand and one attractions. When they are tired of fun and sightseeing there is the popular Carousel to give them zest with rest; the ice cream booth, where they sip cold but delicious comfort; recreation spots galore and the big restaurant with all kinds of nice things to eat and drink.

From a 1909 brochure.

This crowd is waiting for the Go-off in a Long Distance Running event.   The track is rapidly becoming one
of the most popular in this section of the country.

The Race Track, Athletics and the Big Fair in October

NO feature within the fifty acres of ground included within the limits of Olympic Park has made a stronger appeal to the multitude than the half-mile race-track and athletic field, constructed two years ago at a cost of over $25,000. The track, its grand stand seating about 5,000 persons, and its other accessories, are in constant use, during the outdoor season, for field days, horse shows, trotting and running races and other interesting events.   Athletes use them for training grounds, the headquarters of the Olympic Athletic Club being located here, and driving clubs and horsemen in general have season accommodations for their horses in the ample stables and use the track daily.

SPORTING EVENTS AT OLYMPIC PARK

From a 1909 brochure.

33

The Big Dance Hall and Some Other Popular Features

TENS of thousands of the younger generation who worship at the shrine of Terpsichore, patron goddess of the dance, are familiar with the charms of Olympic Park's big ball room. On its 10,000 square feet of floor space gather each afternoon and evening during the outing season such merry throngs of pretty girls and sturdy specimens of young American manhood as it would be well worth travelling many miles to see. The building is 90 by 238 feet in ground dimensions and equipped with every facility for the comfort and convenience of its guests. There is plenty of room for spectators and there are always many who avail themselves of it. Concerts are given by an Orchestra every afternoon and evening. The dance floor is kept in the pink of condition.

¶ But one cannot dance always, and the youthful pleasure-loving spirit sometimes seeks more rollicking amusement. In this line, what better and more harmless than the Roller Toboggan, with its whirl of excitement; the Helter-Skelter, a never failing source of fun and merriment for the children; the Carousel, as popular a form of amusement to-day as it was when the greyheads were young. ¶ And there is the Midway, with its surprises.

¶ Every afternoon and evening there is a Free Stage Vaudeville Entertainment in the open air.

¶ On Sundays, and at various times throughout the week, all sorts of big special features are provided. Many of these are in the class of "thrillers." Watch the newspapers for announcements of these and other Olympic Park events.

A DISTINGUISHED AUTOMOBILE PARTY AT OLYMPIC PARK
ONE GOVERNOR, TWO CONGRESSMEN AND OTHER NOTABLES

From a 1909 brochure.

34

IT is the intention of the management to branch out broadly this year in sporting lines and to develop the fine track and inclosure into one of the big racing and athletic centres of the East.

¶ At the end of the regular park season comes the big New Jersey Fair, with its annual meets of ten days and with as high-class a programme of trotting, running and hurdling events and as large and varied a list of good exhibits and attractions in general as can be found at any fair in this section of the country. The dates for 1909 are October 9 to 19, inclusive.

¶ Since the Park was opened, in 1904, it has made a specialty of entertaining societies and other organizations on the occasion of their annual summer outings. There is never any lack of accommodation for pleasure parties. So ample are the Park's facilities that five hundred carriages and automobiles can be nicely accommodated under cover and over 50,000 visitors can be sheltered.

¶ Olympic Park has always been maintained as a high-class resort. Representatives of the rowdy element will not be tolerated. Games of chance and buncombe of any and every sort are tabooed. Only clean and wholesome amusements are permitted and proper sanitary conditions prevail throughout.

¶ The future of Olympic Park is in the hands of its patrons. It has faithfully striven to promote their comfort and further their enjoyment, believing that in this respect their interests are its own. All it asks is a continuance of that generous patronage which has crowned each season with greater successes than any that had been recorded in the past.

From a 1909 brochure.

of "maneuvers, under regular tactics, or fancy drilling [and] athletic events, some of the grotesque order." Tuesday was children's day, Wednesday, farmer's day; Thursday was set aside for the politicians and Friday, for the motorists. The fair ended on Saturday with a gala carnival. County fairs were held at the park in the fall of each year through 1914.

Area horse fanciers made Olympic Park their favorite rendezvous after Schmidt completed a half mile race track and grandstand in 1909. When the Essex County Speedway closed in 1911, the County Road Horse Association moved its races to the park. Held weekly during the season from 1909 to 1914, the harness races drew large crowds, most of whom stayed long into the night after the last race ended, reliving the day's excitement over hot dogs and beer or the finer fare provided in the dining pavilion. Motorcycle races were introduced in 1909. The race track was one of Olympic Park's best drawing cards, rivaling the opera. Said a Newark paper late in 1911: "An afternoon at the races, followed by a dinner at the restaurant, a performance of grand opera

Mr. and Mrs. Paul Klein Sr. and her young brother photographed "aboard" the good ship Olympic, *c. 1914.*

in the theatre and a dance between acts in the pavilion, should make a Labor Day outing at Olympic Park satisfying to any pleasure seeker."

After years of unbroken success, Schmidt's fortunes turned markedly sour as the 1914 season got underway. On June 14, the opera house burned to the ground on the very day the Olympic Park Company was to open the season with a performance of "Naughty Marietta." The fire was discovered about 30 minutes after midnight when flames were seen shooting from the roof of the theatre. Despite the combined efforts of park employees and local firemen, the building was consumed within an hour. Wind-driven embers set fire to the roof of the dance pavilion and grandstand, and for a time the entire resort was threatened. Schmidt, who personally directed the park's own firefighters, lapsed into a coma at the height of the blaze. When he regained consciousness, he was unable to speak. The estimated $50,000 loss was only partially covered by insurance. Although rebuilt within a month's time, the opera house never regained its former popularity.

James A. Beldon, the park's manager since 1912, announced in August 1914 that Schmidt's creditors would meet soon to decide the resort's future. Beldon attributed the park's $90,000 debt to the opera house fire, general business conditions and "the worst weather in years." A month later a committee representing Schmidt's largest creditors, the Irvington National Bank, Nicholas Weber, F.P. Steiner, Christian Kurz, a lumber company, the Becker family and the Home Brewing Co., took over the park's management. According to the committee, the 25-acre park was worth more than $100,000. Olympic's string of bad luck continued through the fall of 1914 when seven straight days of rain turned the County Fair into a sodden fiasco. In December 1914, the County Prosecutor banned prize fights at the resort, choking off the park's most popular post-season attraction. During the next 10 months, Schmidt tried frantically to raise enough money to pay off his creditors. The inevitable end came on August 6, 1915, when he lost the park at a sheriff's sale to the Home Brewing Co., high bidder at $55,000. The brewing company, which had acquired St. Louis' Forest Park Highlands under similar circumstances 19 years earlier, announced that the park would reopen the following spring.

The park's 13th season, the first without Schmidt's guiding genius, was previewed at a gala dinner hosted by Henry A. Guenther, Home's general manager, in April 1916. "An electric tower 200 feet high, which will blaze its illumination many miles in all directions, will be a feature of Olympic Park this

Herbert Baudistel's Olympic Park Orchestra, 1912. Baudistel (second from right, front row), who was Schmidt's nephew, played at Olympic from 1911 to 1937. From 1937 to 1942 he was a member of Basile's band.

season," said the Newark *News.* Fifty thousand dollars worth of improvements were planned, including several new rides, added the paper. The Aborn Opera Co. would return and Hollis E. Cooley, in charge of special events at the Panama-Pacific Exposition in San Francisco, would be the park's new manager. Christian Kurz, Schmidt's former partner, was introduced as Olympic's "proprietor." Less than a month into the season, the dreams of a new Olympic Park turned to ashes. Despite his best efforts, Kurz could not attract the traditional crowds. Despondent, he committed suicide in his quarters above the saloon in June.

Home Brewing Co. purchased Olympic Park to forestall what would otherwise have been a substantial loss. Not interested in owning the amusement park any longer than necessary, the company hired Kurz as its manager in hopes that the resort could be revived, then sold. When Kurz shot himself, Anthony J. and Henry A. Guenther, Home's principal stockholders, were compelled to take a more active role in the resort's management. What was born out of business necessity gradually became a labor of love: The Guenthers were astute businessmen and quick

studies. They soon discovered that they enjoyed running Olympic Park, and were good at it too.

While the Guenthers may well have thought of buying the park eventually, ratification of the Prohibition Amendment in January 1919 probably speeded their decision. On September 24, 1919, four months before the nation went dry, Henry Guenther bought the park from Home Brewing for approximately $100,000. His brother, Anthony, became manager of the resort and later had charge of the pool until his death in March 1934.

The first five seasons under Guenther management were cast in the Schmidt-Kurz mold. "Olympic Park was taken over by new managers Saturday. . .," reported the *News* on June 12, 1916. "The former policy of the park will be carried out in every detail by the new management. The contract with the Aborn Opera Co. for 12 weeks has been renewed and the Aborns will start their season tonight, presenting 'The Chocolate Soldier.' There will be the usual free show daily and Johnny Mack will make a balloon ascension every Sunday."

"High class" vaudeville twice a day on the open-air stage was an Olympic Park tradition the Guenthers were happy to continue. The acts, all of which had to be suitable for family viewing, were of good quality and tended to draw patrons to the park. Herrera, an aerialist who hung by his teeth 90 feet in the air; Marvelous Marlow, the human dragon contortionist; George Trump, a legless high-wire artist; Idaline Colton, "the Flexible Venus;" and Norma, "the Frog-Man," were typical of the period. Others were: McArdle and Doyle, whirlwind dancing demons; Ranch and French, burlesque knockabout comedians; Magnetta, billed as "the woman who defies all efforts to remove her from anything she touches," so popular she was held over for three weeks in 1918; and Professor Charles Douglas, "who without any adventitious aids to verisimilitude, enables his audience to communicate with their friends in spiritland." Dancing goats, mind-reading canines, leaping wolfhounds, trained Bengal tigers and Shetland ponies also delighted audiences. A cage had to be specially built in July 1918 when Captain Scholl displayed his three Nubian lions, Julius, Babe and Prince. The brave captain tempted death twice a day as he rode Prince around the stage and stuck his head in two-year-old Babe's mouth. In 1920, the Guenthers booked a pair of one-ring circuses for their patrons, Hocum's Big London Circus in June, Bostock's European Circus two months later.

The Guenthers worked hard to create an amusement park with something for everyone. A newspaper ad of June 1919 promised nightly dancing, weekend concerts, a playground for the kiddies, side shows, a Niagara Falls of fireworks and something called Karsey's Myriophone, "an instrument containing 2,000 wires. . ." that presumably made music. An article appearing alongside the ad called the park "the favorite pleasure resort for families. On week days, mothers leave their children to romp in the playground, which is free, and on Sundays fathers, mothers and little ones picnic on the grounds amid beautiful flowers and the musical accompaniment of Vincentz's band."

Park patrons could choose from an endless variety of amusements. The Aborn Opera Co., featuring recent Broadway musicals along with the tried and true operettas of Herbert, Friml and Gilbert and Sullivan, played to packed houses. A downtown ticket office in Firemen's Pharmacy at Broad and Market Streets promoted sales and children accompanied by adults could attend the Saturday and Sunday matinees for only a dime. Sunday afternoon dinners in the restaurant were still 75 cents. "A feature of Olympic Park is the Sunday dinner, which is so satisfactory and so moderately priced as to induce families to spend the whole day at the park, instead of first taking the meal at home." The dance hall could accommodate 3,500. Professor Vincentz's 20-piece band played nightly and on Saturdays afternoons, attracting "large numbers of votaries of terpsichore to the wonderful Olympic Park floor." Wednesday was souvenir night, with prizes awarded to the best dancers. On Sundays, when the dance hall was closed, Vincentz's and Guenther's bands played

The Rustic Bridge, c. 1910, from an old postcard.

ABOVE — *The pathway leading to the Opera House. Paths were covered with cinders and gravel.* BELOW — *The main entrance and 43rd Street trolley loop, c. 1915. Those who arrived by carriage or automobile could park their vehicles in covered and attended sheds.*

sacred concerts in the picnic grove. Other amusements were a bowling alley, shooting gallery, Japanese rolling-stand, merry-go-round, race track and baseball diamond. Children under 12 were admitted free.

Olympic Park remained a favorite locale for club outings, veteran's reunions, political rallies, public school graduations and, after World War I broke out, patriotic gatherings and dinners honoring departing soldiers. On April 28, 1918, the Guenthers threw open the park to Irvington residents in honor of the 313th Regiment, then en route from Fort Dix to the European battlefront. Two months later Olympic was again free to townspeople when the Blue Devils, a company of 100 highly-decorated French soldiers on tour in America, stopped at the park to boost the sale of War Savings Stamps. An estimated 10,000 crammed the resort to honor men who, as the local paper put it, "faced and defeated the desperate onslaughts of the Hun in the trenches of Flanders."

"Aside from the girls there was one thing in the park that seemed to captivate them," continued the paper. "The entertainment committee had provided an elaborate lunch with the popular French wine. The only 'faim' they felt was hunger from the thrilling sensations of the 'loop-the-loop.' The dips and dives of that machine delighted them. It was all the committee could do to get half of them inside the restaurant for the dinner."

With the return of peace, John Philip Sousa resumed his national tours, making his first post-war appearance at the park on June 15, 1919. Sousa's 60-piece band, the country's finest, played before standing-room-only crowds. High point of the concert was a quintet of Sousa's own marches, "Bullets and Bayonets," "The Golden Star," "Sabers and Spurs," "Semper Fidelis" and the March King's stirring "Stars and Stripes Forever."

One of the park's finest traditions was the annual orphan outing. "Hundreds of youngsters had the time of their life at Olympic Park yesterday," said *The Clinton Weekly* in June 1920. "Incidentally, scores of autoists had a pretty good time themselves over the happiness which fairly oozed from the kiddies. . . . Flag-decorated cars filled with from three to a dozen riotous youngsters made a pretty sight as the long procession of autos passed through the town to the park where the boys and girls were guests for the day."

5

FOR THE PLEASURE OF ITS PATRONS

Manager Hans Wevers' July 1904 announcement that comic opera would be substituted for vaudeville in the rustic semi-open air threatre launched 16 consecutive seasons of the finest entertainment ever presented in northern New Jersey. The opera company, said Wevers, would be under the direction of Milton and Sargent Aborn who, he added, "have earned an excellent reputation for well-doing in this form of entertainment. The company is not simply a summer-snap organization, formed to play in suburban resorts during the hot weather months. It exists all the year around, and has a regular clientele in the different cities visited by it during the regular season. It has a large repertoire of standard comic operas, by such composers as Audran, Milloecker, Strauss, Lecocq, Planquette, Offenbach and Gilbert and Sullivan, and carries all the scenery and properties needful for the effective presentation of the operettas in which it appears."

Robert Planquette's "The Chimes of Normandy," a French comic opera "in which the romantic sentiment and the droll humor are as pleasing as the melodious music," was Aborn's premier offering, starring comedian Robert Lett, Grace Orr Myers, a sprightly comedienne, Ethel Houston Du Fre, contralto, Annie Myers, Joseph W. Smith, Frank Wooley and Edward Chapman, with a chorus of 30 and a "capable orchestra" under the direction of Carl Burton. When standing-room-only opera crowds affirmed the wisdom of his decision, Manager Wevers

extended the season to September, with a different production each week. After "The Chimes of Normandy" came "The Bohemian Girl" by Balfe, Auber's "Fra Diavolo," "The Mikado" by Gilbert and Sullivan, von Flotow's "Martha," "Girofle Girofla," a French opera bouffe by Lecocq, Victor Herbert's "The Fortune Teller" and William Wallace's "Maritana," one of the first operas written in English. So popular were the shows that after the regular troupe departed on the balance of its tour, the Aborns put together a pastiche of scenes from "Faust," "Cavalleria Rusticana" and "Il Trovatore." The 1905 season closed in the grand style with a production of Verdi's masterpiece, "Il Trovatore," given in its entirety with chorus members drawn from New York's Metropolitan Opera House.

Bringing opera to Olympic Park was a bold stroke by Schmidt, Kurz and Wevers, himself a former singer and manager at German opera houses, but it was one that paid off handsomely for many years. It immediately distinguished the park from its competition, which continued to feature Wild West shows and vaudeville exclusively, and quickly attracted a "better class" of patrons who stayed longer and spent more. Explained a local newspaper: "Only a short time elapsed before it began to be the fashion to attend the operatic performances and long before the season closed the spectacle of many automobiles carrying parties from all points of the compass to the park was a nightly occurrence. . . . The character of

ABOVE — *The Aborn Opera Company, 1908.* BELOW — *A capacity crowd fills the original opera house, 1908. Rebuilt after a 1914 fire, the opera house served in later years as a funhouse, dance hall (with a Chinese restaurant and bowling alleys beneath it) and, finally, a skating rink.*

the musical offerings was reflected in the character of the audiences, which greatly differed in aspect from that of those patronizing suburban resorts where the entertainment provided appeals less strongly to persons of musical and cultural taste. So well liked were the performances that hundreds of persons made a point of being present at some one of the representations each week." Added the paper: "Manager Wevers early let the fact be understood that any unseemly behavior within the park would not be tolerated, and the freedom from annoyance of any kind. . . helped to promote the pleasure of the patrons."

In short order, Olympic Park became a mecca for summertime pleasure seekers. People in horse and buggy or the new-fangled baby gas wagons came early to enjoy the rides or a fine meal in the restaurant before taking their seats in the spacious theatre. When the performance ended the crowds strolled the lighted groves or danced till the wee hours in the open-air pavilion. No other amusement park in the area offered such a variety of entertainment.

Without the Aborn Light Opera Co., Olympic Park's musical offerings would have been far less successful. America's foremost repertory company, it featured comic and light opera performed entirely in English. The casts were first-rate, the staging, costumes and scenery of the highest quality. A stage director and leading comedian of the Keith-Albee vaudeville circuit in his early years, Milton Aborn (1864-1933) formed his own touring company at the turn of the century. With his brother Sargent (1867-1956), he later established a circuit of companies which presented grand and comic opera in 12 cities from 1902 to 1911 and again after 1915. Gilbert and Sullivan, Victor Herbert, Friml and Kern were Aborn mainstays; Italian and French grand opera and German and French light romantic opera completed their repertoire. Broadway hits were added later.

When the second season of opera began on May 26, 1906, with a performance of Audran's operetta, "La Mascotte," further renovations greeted park patrons. Mosquito netting screened the open-air restaurant, there was a small lake between the theatre and the merry-go-round and the flower beds had been enlarged "in a manner that will add to the picturesqueness of the grove and lawns." The theatre was much improved, with windows that could be closed in the event of rain, dressing rooms, a new roof and the old hard seats replaced by roomy cane opera chairs. There were now 1,000 reserved seats "at slightly higher prices" and hundreds of others "within the reach of very slender purses." These improvements, said the Newark News, made the thea-

Milton Aborn

tre "one of the most commodious and comfortable play houses to be found at a suburban resort." Offerings of the 12-week season included Offenbach's "La Perichole," "The Pirates of Penzance" and "The Mikado" by Gilbert and Sullivan, von Suppe's "Boccaccio," "Maritana," Johann Strauss' "The Merry War," "The Black Hussar" and "The Beggar Student" by Milloecker, Stahl's "Said Pasha" and Auber's "Fra Diavolo." A mid-July double bill featured "Cavalleria Rusticana" and "H.M.S. Pinafore." Lead performers under the baton of Howard Cook were Fritzi von Busing, Robinson Newbold, Robert Lett, Edith Bradford and Frank Wooley, who doubled as stage manager.

Successive seasons featured an amazingly varied repertoire that included Kerker's "The Belle of New York" and "The Telephone Girl," von Suppe's "Boccaccio," "El Capitan" by John Philip Sousa, Bizet's "Carmen," Victor Herbert's "The Fortune Teller," "It Happened in Nordland," "The Serenade" and "The Wizard of the Nile," Verdi's "Il Trovatore," De Koven's "Robin Hood," a favorite of Olympic Park audiences, "H.M.S. Pinafore," "The Mikado" and a string of lesser works now long forgotten.

In 1911, the Aborns introduced a number of new

A Scene From "MLLE. MODISTE" at Olympic Park

productions including "King Dodo" with Robert Lett as "the jolly old potentate of Spoojuland," "Little Johnny Jones" by George M. Cohan, Victor Herbert's "Mlle. Modiste" and "The Red Mill." Stars that year were Ada Meade, Robinson Newbold, Blanche Morrison, Robert Lett, Agnes Finlay and Olga von Hatzfeldt. After the season ended with "H.M.S. Pinafore," the Aborns sent in their English Grand Opera Co. for a two-week engagement that featured Puccini's "Madame Butterfly," "The Tales of Hoffman" by Offenbach and Massenet's "Thais."

Olympic Park's ninth season of opera began on June 2, 1912, without the Aborn company, disbanded when the Aborn brothers formed a New York-based touring company dedicated to the production of grand opera in English. With the loss of the Aborns, Schmidt turned to a succession of promoters, including Frank M. Rainger and Franklin Baggot, who took the reins in 1913.

The Olympic Park Opera Company offered many of the same operas as the Aborns had featured and some of the same performers. New productions seen at the park included Cohan's "George Washington Jr.," "The Gondoliers" by Gilbert and Sullivan, "Die Fledermaus," Philipp's "Alma, Where Do You Live," another park favorite, and "Quincy Adams Sawyer," billed as "a rattling good play of country life, bright, fresh and breezy and filled with honest love and romance, country songs, barn dances, Virginia reels, husking bees and other lively events that mark country life in New England today." Blanche Morrison, Ferne Rogers and Laura Jaffray were featured performers. Members of the cast did double duty in the restaurant before and after the curtain, singing and dancing the best numbers from the show. When "The Mikado" was staged, the park's staff dressed in oriental costume.

A spectacular fire destroyed the theatre barely 24 hours before the 1914 season was to open with a performance of "Naughty Marietta." Seen for miles around, the blaze quickly reduced the playhouse to a pile of charred timbers, consuming scenery, costumes and the personal effects of the 40-member cast. Undaunted by the disaster, the company transferred its operations to the Newark Theatre, performing there until a new theatre could be built. Less than a month later, on July 11, a new opera house was dedicated with a performance of "The Wedding Day," a comic opera starring Blanche Rae Edwards, James Mc Elhern and Hattie Arnold. "The size of the gathering and the reception given the singers," said the Newark News, "indicated that such operatic entertainment as is provided at this suburban yet easily accessible resort is appreciated by many lovers of operetta and musical comedy." In general appearance, Schmidt's new theatre resembled the old,

44

Maude Leekley

Fritzi von Busing

A scene from The Fortune Teller, *1907.*

but it was somewhat smaller, with a seating capacity of 1,600. Removal of the support columns which had made many seats in the former auditorium undesirable was a welcome improvement.

The fire that reduced the playhouse to rubble virtually ruined the 1914 season. Attendance, which had been gradually dropping off since 1912, now plummeted. Reviews of Olympic Park Opera Company productions were less than enthusiastic, adding to Schmidt's growing troubles. He persevered, however, opening the 1915 season on July 5 with a performance of Auber's popular comic opera, "Fra Diavolo." A company of 36 singers under the direction of W.B. Shackford performed but four weeks before slumping patronage forced the cancellation of opera at the park.

When Christian Kurz agreed to manage the park for the Home Brewing Co. after Schmidt's bank-ruptcy, he refurbished the theatre, signed a contract with the Aborn brothers and crossed his fingers. After a four-year absence, the Aborn Opera Co. returned to Olympic Park on June 12, 1916, beginning a 12-week engagement with Straus' comic opera, "The Chocolate Soldier." Opening week's standing-room-only audiences reversed the park's fortunes. With their well-known singers and polished performances, the Aborns soon brought the old crowds flocking back to Olympic Park. "Olympic Park has come into its own," said a Newark newspaper, "and the Aborn Opera Co. has demonstrated that music lovers will patronize first-class productions of the late Broadway successes when given in so capable a manner." Saturday and Sunday matinees were scheduled along with seven evening performances. Tickets were 25 cents for children, 50 and 75 cents for adults. Eileen Castles, the Australian

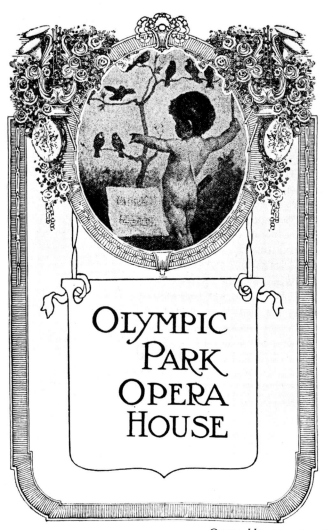

Opera House program, week of July 3, 1916.

"Pleading guilty to charges of being a bunch of 'gourmands,' some 50 men, prominent throughout the State, were locked up in an improvised jail in the dining-room of Olympic Park last night," reported The Clinton Weekly *on May 7, 1915. "Forced to don prison garb and under the eyes of Warden Hosp of the county penitentiary, the prisoners were given the kind of jail food as might be served on a holiday. The diners were members of the Police Chiefs' Association of New Jersey, which held a session here yesterday.... The interior of the dining-room was hung with canvas painted to represent the interior of a prison eating-room. Gratings covered the windows. A long, low table was set with ordinary prison fare, and the diners sat on long wooden benches. The plates, knives and forks were used, all articles being chained to the table in approved fashion. Each diner wore a cap and coat made by inmates of the Caldwell penitentiary. Guards watched as they ate." Herman Schmidt, dressed as a warden, looks on approvingly.*

prima donna, Mildred Rogers, Fritzi von Busing, her husband, Forrest Huff, and Robinson Newbold starred in well-known works by Herbert, Friml and Gilbert and Sullivan. "Naughty Marietta," Herbert's sprightly operetta, closed the season. Rhapsodized one newsman: "How many. . .realize that a delightful trolley ride through the country of about half an hour, with the range of the beautiful Orange Mountains always in view, will bring them to the Olympic Park Opera House. . .? So wake up, Mr. Commuter. Be refreshed by a good laugh and cheered by delightful music, as necessary as bread in these days of overwork and nervous tension."

Gradually audiences began to turn away from European opera in favor of Broadway revivals. The Aborns accommodated the demand for "ultra-modern compositions" in 1918 with productions of "Very Good Eddie," by Jerome Kern, "Flora Belle," "Sergeant Kitty," "A Modern Eve" and "The Lilac Domino," billed as a "sparkling comedy [with] situations now verging upon the spicey, now filled with the glamor of romance or the wistfulness of tears."

After the war, public taste began to change again. Summer theatre was less popular and the crowds at the Olympic Park playhouse thinned noticeably. From an artistic standpoint, the 1919 and 1920 sea-

Olympic Park advertised heavily in the Evening News *as well as in Newark's German-language press, which in those days enjoyed a wide circulation throughout New Jersey.*

sons were as good as any the Aborn Company had staged at the park. De Koven's "Robin Hood" opened the 1920 season, followed by Herbert's "Sweethearts" and "Naughty Marietta," "The Red Mill" and "Oh Boy," a Jerome Kern musical featuring such then popular songs as "A Package of Seeds," "Flubby-Dub," "Cave Man," "Oh, Daddy Please" and "Till The Clouds Roll By." Casts included Maude Gray, Eva Quintard, Ottilie Corday, Phil Branson, John Phillips and the park's all-time favorites, Forrest Huff and Fritzi von Busing. "Alma, Where Do You Live," which began a run of 10 performances on Labor Day, was the final offering.

Henry Guenther's decision to convert the theatre into a funhouse marked the end of opera at Olympic Park. In February 1922, local newspapers reported that Guenther was negotiating with the Aborns to revive the performances on a large open air stage erected within the race track oval, but the plans failed to materialize. A vestige of an earlier, less hectic era, the gentle summertime laughter and lilting music of light opera in the park had fallen victim to the fast-paced Roaring Twenties.

6

QUITE A PLACE IN ITS DAY

When Herman Schmidt and Christian Kurz opened Olympic Park's new half-mile harness racing track in May 1909, they added another chapter to a story that began the day the Hilton Base Ball Club first took the field at Becker's Grove nearly a quarter-century before. To three generations of New Jersey sports enthusiasts, Olympic Park meant far more than scary rides and free circus acts. The thousands of fans who came each year to watch boxing bouts, bicycle races, waterpolo matches, football, baseball and basketball games, automobile races, soccer matches, the trotters and a host of other events staged at the park would have been quick to agree with Willie Ratner's assessment of Olympic Park's unique place in New Jersey sports annals. "It was quite a place in its day," wrote the longtime Newark *News* sports reporter. "Olympic Park was the only amusement park in the East that traditionally offered patrons a wide variety of sporting events of more than ordinary local interest."

Profits from Olympic's phenomenally successful early years, plus a hefty bank loan, made it possible for Schmidt and Kurz to build the racetrack, a paddock for the trotters and pacers and a block-long covered wooden grandstand that seated 2,500. Races were held on Saturday afternoons from June to October annually until 1913 when waning attendance forced the track's closing. In its heyday, however, Decoration Day, Fourth of July, Labor Day and Columbus Day meets drew crowds of 4,000 or

more. In an era when many a family still owned its own horse (and those of means owned two or three or more), harness racing was a popular gentlemen's sport. Owners raced their horses themselves, or, like A.C. Hensler and Frederick Ballantine, employed professional trainers to take the reins. Olympic Park's meets were sponsored by both the New Jersey and Essex County Road Horse Associations, which numbered among their members many of the state's wealthiest men. For years Weequahic Park's Waverly track and the Essex County Speedway in Irvington had drawn scores of amateur racers on weekends. When the Olympic Park track opened, its superior facilities quickly made it the area's most popular course. "In former years the Waverly track was used almost daily by the horsemen in preparing their animals for the racing season," wrote the Newark *News* in 1909. "This year the scene has changed and most of the horses are being trained at the Olympic Park track. As many as 40 horses are being worked out every day at the Olympic track and many of the horses that were stabled in former years at Waverly are among them. . . . At the Olympic Park track it is not an uncommon sight to see as many as 15 to 20 horses on the track at one time. The railbirds who used to congregate at the Waverly track and clock the horses have changed their headquarters to the new track and can be seen there with regularity, timing the speed merchants." Spectators who paid to sit in the grandstand or line up along the

A view of the paddock, from a postcard. The Merry-Go-Round is to the right.

"A Close Finish on the Race Track," looking to the northeast.

Gas Buggies and horse-drawn carriages crowd the parking lot on race day.

board fence that encircled the track were forbidden by law from betting on the outcome of the races, a prohibition few honored.

Light harness racing at Olympic Park became a relic of the past in 1914 when Schmidt disclosed plans to build a large swimming pool at the northeast end of the track. When that project fell through for lack of interest, he constructed a quarter-mile running track for athletic events in front of the old grandstand, using the home stretch of the track for the start and finish line. The new track was first used on June 12, 1914, when the Prudential Athletic Assn. staged its annual games at the park.

On July 24, 1915, the novelty of automobile racing came to Olympic Park as a large field of professional drivers competed in 14 events on the former harness track, half of the races held after dark "under the glare of a huge night lighting plant brought here from Brighton Beach." The main event was a 100-mile race, with cash prizes totalling $5,000. "A 10-foot canvas wall will encircle the entire track," reported *The Clinton Weekly*, "and will act as a huge reflector for the myriad of powerful lamps placed. . . every 25 feet around the course. The racing cars silhouetted against the white canvas wall can be seen as plainly as in the daytime." Roy Repp, the Australian trick auto driver, and his "wonder car" entertained the fans before the races. "His trained auto,

The 2.25 pacers cross the finish line in front of the grandstand, Memorial Day 1909. Races were held on Memorial Day, the Fourth of July and Labor Day.

Doctor Bill, owned by a Dr. Mitchell, from the Newark Evening News, 1909.

Highland Laddie wins the 2.27 trot, Labor Day 1909.

The Home-Stretch, Olympic Park, Newark, N. J.

"The Home-Stretch," from an old postcard.

Little Bill finishes first in the 2.25 pace, 1909.

as Repp calls it, rears up on its rear wheels, spins round like a top on two wheels, bucks like a bronco, and, in fact, does everything except talk." More than 4,000 people watched the July 24 extravaganza, the largest crowd seen at Olympic Park since the glory days of the Aborn Opera Co.

Encouraged by their success, the park staged additional Saturday races during the 1915 season, the last on September 6 when 3,500 cheered Brooklyn's Ira Vail as he swept the field. Behind the wheel of a Mulford Special built especially for the October Astor Cup race, Vail won first place in five of the six races, taking first money and prizes in the one-mile time trials, three races of three miles each and a special three-mile handicap. "Only once did the Brooklyn pilot find it necessary to drive his car at full speed," reported the New York Times. "This happened in the three-mile handicap, when Vail overcame big time handicaps and defeated Joe Jackson, who drove a Correja. It looked as if Vail would make a clean sweep of the card until he burst a tire in the fourth mile of the Australian pursuit race. . . ." Another racer, Bert Duryea, sent his Ford Special crashing into the fence at the dangerous north curve. John DePalma, Ralph's brother, started in two of the races before he withdrew when his "machine" developed gearbox trouble.

Auto racing continued to be a top attraction at Olympic Park in 1916 and 1917, drawing some of the nation's finest drivers, among them Ralph DePalma, Harold Alexander, who held the track record, Louis and Gaston Chevrolet and Ira Vail. In April 1916, the Olympic Park Racing Assn. was formed to conduct a regular schedule of races at the track under the sanction of the American Automobile Assn. Elimination of the perilous north curve, demanded by the AAA, made the course safer but far less spectacular. Christian Kurz, president of the racing association, unveiled a large trophy featuring a silver tire and winged foot to be presented to the driver with the season's largest point score.

Racing began on Decoration Day with a six-race program that saw Bert Watson, driving a J.J.R. Special, Joe Dickinson in a Stutz Special and George Theobald behind the wheel of a Mercedes take first, second and third place, respectively. The first night race on July 17 drew a crowd of 3,000 to watch Joe Dickinson drive a 100-horsepower Stutz to a new track record of 37 and 3/5th seconds. The evening's biggest thrill came when a $10,000 Sunbeam driven by Theobald caught fire seconds after it crossed the finish line. "Theobald had just circled the half-mile track when sparks were seen coming from the radiator," said the News. "Within a few seconds, the en-

tire front of the car was enveloped in fire and Theobald was still in his seat. With presence of mind he kept his machine on the track, applying the brakes for all he was worth in the meanwhile. With one shoe ablaze, Theobald finally jumped."

The 1917 season opened on May 30 when Dickinson, then the track record-holder, won five of the six races on the program in his powerful Stutz before 4,000 excited fans. "His combination of nerve, skill on a half-mile dirt track and 100-horsepower Stutz was just too much for the contenders," reported the News.

"Dickinson furnished the first real thrill of the day in the time trials at one-half mile by sweeping around the bumpy curves in a yellow dirt cloud in 35 and 1/5 seconds, which was one-fifth of a second lower than the record made July 4 last year when he and Barber tied for the honor. His other time-smashing stunt was in the Australian pursuit race. . . ."

"It was apparent during the time trials at a half-mile, the first event on the program, that Dickinson's car was in perfect condition and that he intended to take chances. The track was somewhat dusty and rough on the first and the three-quarter turns, but this didn't worry him. Roland C. Gifford in a Gif-Ford special, a reconstructed Ford, had made the best time, 40 and 1/5th seconds until Dickinson came on the track. . . ."

"Five cars went into the three-mile non-stock race for cars 300 cubic inches and under. The little Gif-Ford took the lead from the start and held it, although challenged twice on the stretches by the Mercer. The pace was a little too swift for the Maxwell and it dropped out at two miles, leaving the Mercer and Gif-Ford to fight it out with an Elgin Special a bad third. . . ."

The racing grew more exciting as the program proceeded. "In the five-mile race with seven entries, Dickinson shot away to a lead almost instantly and going down the back-stretch had a 100-yard gap between himself and Gifford. George Dolan in a 100 horsepower Buick, a relic of the last Vanderbilt cup race, with side exhaust pipes for every cylinder, thundered along a close third on the first lap. At a mile and one-half Gifford tried to creep up on Dickinson but the Cranford man shot into the turn to the right of the grandstand at such a terrific clip that both were completely lost to view in the dirt. Jessop in the Mercer and George Theobald were fighting it out for last place. On this lap, Theobald swept by Jessop, the Elgin and a Stutz driven by Ralph Snyder. At two miles he challenged the juggernaut Buick on the back stretch and they skidded into the home stretch side by side. Before the third mile Theobald made a desperate effort to get by Gifford but the latter had his little boat under perfect control on the turns and it was so light it didn't seem to skid like the big cars. Jessop and Snyder see-sawed all the way through the third mile and took all kinds of chances trying to get by each other. Jessop finally won out and held fourth place to the finish."

"In the meantime," continued the *News* account, "Theobald had quit on the back stretch and the battle was between Gifford and Dolan for second place. On the last lap Dolan turned loose everything there was left in the big Buick and went into the final turn almost abreast of the little white Gif-Ford. With a sweep that brought the crowd up standing, they came into home stretch abreast with the Buick on the outside, and it wasn't until they were within 50 yards of the finish line that Dolan succeeded in forging to the front for second place. Dickinson finished a good 100 yards in the lead."

Before the first race, Essex County auto dealers paraded their latest floor models around the track.

The holiday crowd applauded with delight as a procession of brightly polished cars that included a Haynes, Dodge, National, Packard, Hudson, Paige and Saxon, Chalmers, Stutz, Chevrolet, Stanley Steamer, Maxwell and Peerless moved slowly past the grandstand. The war in Europe cast its lengthening shadow over the races when "an automobile load of officers joined in the parade preceeding the auto races. . . ." According to the papers, "recruiting forces" were highly visible at the park and "soldiers were plentiful in the crowd."

Racing continued as scheduled in 1917 before being suspended in 1918 and 1919 due to the wartime gasoline shortage. During the 1920 season, six races were held every Saturday. The Columbus Day race, in which Ira Vail captured all seven meets he entered, was marred by the track's first serious accident. During the half-mile time trial, a driver was badly injured when his car climbed over a 30-foot embankment at the center of the first curve. The car turned a somersault, catapulting the driver 40 feet

BELOW — *Roy Repp's "wonder car" did everything but talk, according to press accounts, July 1915. More than 4,000 spectators jammed the stands.*

LEFT — *Walter Goerke and*, ABOVE — *Percy Drummond led the mayhem on the half-mile dirt track, 1909.*

into heavy underbrush.

Sports fans were treated to another form of organized mayhem in September 1909 when the N.J. Motorcycle Club, headquartered in Newark, began a series of Saturday meets on the half-mile dirt track. Held during September and October from 1909 to 1911, the motorcycle races featured a variety of hair-raising contests, including competitions for single and double-cylinder machines, team relay matches, three, five and 15-mile handicaps and a five-mile scratch race. A match between a bicycle rider and a motorcycle and one in which contestants ran 50 yards to the starting line, mounted their machines, then rode to within 50 yards of the finish, dismounted and finished on foot, were among the novelty races enjoyed by fans. Howard O'Brien, Roy Pascall, described by the press as "practically fearless," Percy

Drummond, Walter Goerke, John Constant, America's 10-mile champion, and Frank Hart, the national champion, were track regulars.

Boxing matches in the Olympic Park ballroom under the aegis of the Olympic Athletic Club were first held in 1914. Jim Savage fought Sailor Burke there and Jimmie McVeigh, Banty Lewis, Mickey Donley and Eddie Nugent pounded their opponents before appreciative crowds. Since state law permitted boxing bouts but not prize fighting, members of the County Prosecutor's staff attended most fights to monitor compliance. Four fights held at the park in the fall of 1914 drew an average attendance of 1,000 before the Prosecutor called a halt to the matches in December. An effort to resume the fights two years later met with stiff resistance from town authorities and a warning from the Prosecutor that he would arrest the promoters. In December 1920, Eddie Nugent, a middleweight contender, floored Bob Gleason of New York in the first round of a four-bout card sanctioned by the State Boxing Commission. Young Pep, Soldier Bill Hines, Jack Williams and Kid Kabilis, all well-known local boxers, also appeared. Public sentiment against "the manly art" and the antagonism of Irvington police officials prevented the development of a regular program of boxing at the park and, following the Nugent-Gleason fight, professional bouts were discontinued for good.

Boxing was revived in September 1938 when a month-long series of charity bouts were held at the

Roy Pascall, 1910.

vington Blue Sox, the famed Tuscan Farmers and the Cardinals, a local team coached by Dr. Maclyn Baker. Irvington High School played its home games at the stadium in the late Twenties and early Thirties as well.

In the late Twenties, the roller skating rink echoed to the crack of bats when Hal Chase led a group of American and National League stars in an indoor baseball game, a sport in which many big leaguers used to participate in the off-season.

Fans in 1930 were treated to the bewhiskered House of David nine, a team said to be "on a par with the big league stars" but whose religious beliefs kept them from "the big time," and Josie Caruso, "the greatest female baseball star in the history of the national pastime," and "Her Eight Men." The only woman on the team, Josie played first base, managed and batted "as well as any man."

Henry Guenther introduced the excitement of midget auto racing to New Jersey sports enthusiasts in the summer of 1934. "Thrills and spills are fast-happening features of the new sport, popular for two years on the West Coast," reported the local press. "Midget cars have a 66 to 75-inch wheel-base, a wheel rim diameter of 10 to 12 inches, [are] brake

circus grounds to raise money for underprivileged children. "The bouts also will give local youngsters, many of whom probably believe themselves of championship timber, an opportunity to see what they can do with their dukes," reported the Irvington *Herald.* George Moir, the state's amateur heavyweight champion, and "stern-faced" Steve Sneigocki, dubbed the "Pulverizing Pole," headlined the benefit matches, just one of the many charity events underwritten by Henry Guenther.

Local baseball teams played on the Olympic diamond from April to October before enthusiastic crowds, but the games were only a sideshow until 1927 when Guenther teamed up with Henry "Casey" Glossen, the veteran pilot of Newark's old Ironside team, to bring semi-pro ball to Olympic Park and make it a paying proposition. Guenther invested $50,000 in a new stadium, bleachers and a modern diamond on land he acquired along 40th Street. The ball park had its own entrance and, when the games were over, patrons were admitted to the amusement area free of charge. For his part, Glossen, who in past years had brought a parade of Japanese, Chinese and Cuban teams to Newark, lined up the best semi-pro talent for the park. Among the semi-pro teams that called the Olympic Park stadium home during the Twenties and Thirties were the Ir-

Margaret Gould, 1910.

Thomas A. Edison and his employees crowded Olympic Park for the annual Edison Field Day, June 12, 1913. Admission was 25¢. A one dollar ticket included a full course dinner in the restaurant after the games. Edison himself is visible at lower left and lower right wearing a black hat with a flat crown.

Coach McNally shows his S.A.L. baseball team how it's done, 1939.

equipped and have a fire-proof wall between engine and driver with a road clearance of four inches. Cars speed as high as 50 miles per hour. . . . Thrill seekers will see five five-lap races, a 15-lap and a 30-lap event on the program." According to the papers, leading West Coast riders would compete against the best midget auto drivers of the East on the park's one-fifth mile dirt track.

The Sunday afternoon races, usually featuring 30 to 35 entries, were noisy, fast-paced and extremely hazardous to both drivers and machines, at least until 1935 when the track was coated with cinders for better traction. In 1934, Emil Knab, driving a Citroen Special, suffered serious internal injuries following a spectacular crash. Two years later, Walter Fusco barely escaped with his life when his midget racer went up in flames after a gas line snapped.

In the spring of 1936, the races, now under the sponsorship of the Metropolitan Motor Racing Assn., were rescheduled to Monday evenings, immediately raising the hackles of nearby residents who complained bitterly about the annoying noise and dust. Bowing to public pressure, Guenther dropped the midget car corps from his list of attractions before summer's end. Bill Troutwine, the Florida state champion, held the track record for 20 laps in a hair under six minutes. Other drivers who risked life and limb on the mini-track were Mac Mackenzie, Wild Bill Lawrence, Beany Jann, Wild Bill Holmes, "Milk Wagon" Smith and George Krantz, the point winner in 1936.

7

OLYMPIC PARK
MADE NEWS

*Olympic Park made news from the day John Becker
threw open the gates to his picnic grove in 1887. During
the park's heyday its publicity staff churned out 50 or
more articles and pictures a season. Local newsmen
found the place a delightfully dependable source of
colorful feature stories.*

Sunday Amber Mining

Becker's Grove presented a lively scene yesterday. Hundreds of people were there, participating in a big Sunday jollification and the emptying of innumerable kegs of beer.

It was the occasion of the fifth annual May ride of the Five Finger Club and the members had made preparations for its celebration so elaborate in detail that the High License law had no terror for them. Beer in unlimited quantities was essential to the success of the affair. The committee of arrangements assessed each male member $2, and each woman $1 for shares in the stock of edibles and beverages to be consumed on the grounds . . . .

Accompanied by a number of musicians, the "shareholders" and their families drove in stages and trucks to the grove and staked their claim. The Central Penny Club of this city was also present in large numbers, and a little breeze as to which crowd should have full possession arose. Mr. Becker said that all parties could remain and have a good time. The Five Finger contingent secured a long rope and marked off their territory to the exclusion of the others.

The Central Penny delegation had its band of musicians along, and in retaliation took possession of the dancing pavilion, and none of the other club's delegation, except the girls, were permitted to dance. In order to obtain beer from the Five Finger crowd it was necessary to have a badge indicating that the wearer had paid his proper footing, and was part owner in the product of the amber mine.

Money could not buy a drink, but members of the Hilton Base Ball Club and a party from Protection Hose Co. Number 1, of Elizabeth, who came later and set up kegs of beer, generously allowed all comers to help themselves.

Two ball matches were played. The Hiltons defeated the Elizabeth fire laddies by the score of 10 to 1. Captain Heer's and Captain Leary's teams, made up of Five Finger members, played a ten-inning game, which resulted in a tie—22 to 22.

When the Elizabeth men's beer ran out they advanced on the bar of the Five Finger Club and insisted that lager be sold to them. As the applicants for beer refused to be shaken off, a fight followed, in which several members of both sides were severely bruised. The Five Finger warriors succeeded in defending their kegs.

Newark *Evening News*
May 28, 1888

Olympic Park Opens

Ever since last summer when a large amusement park, indeed the largest that Newark has ever seen, opened nearby, our city has been the richer. Now, the park's second season is about to begin; and it will be evident to all that the park management has spared no expense to do justice to the public in every possible way.

On May 27, the second season of the new, and in many respects enlarged and improved Olympic Park, will open. When the hot days of June, July and August approach on the wings of summer's heat and humidity, Olympic Park, with its heaven-high shade trees and cool grounds, will be a veritable paradise for city-folks.

A paradise full of pleasure! For months we have been hearing of the momentous preparations underway at this most beautiful place of recreation on the heights of Hilton, where rich promenades decorated with countless festive blossoms present a striking appearance at all hours of the day and night.

Olympic Park is the pearl of all summer gardens! During the hottest days of summer, its healthful climate and refreshing breezes are a tonic.

A highlight is the evening concert in an illuminated setting reminiscent of The Thousand and One Nights. It is a garden setting in the best style, with an abundance of the most rare imported trees and shrubs, all bound together in a harmonious whole; where tasteful waterworks such as fountains and springs bubble with life, and out of the dark green of the shrubbery shimmer white statues, the taste of the artist adding to the beauty of nature.

At Olympic Park the art of the electric light achieves a blinding effect: There, a dark path winds through countless festoons glowingly lighted with electricity; here, an open grassy area; there, under the falling drops of the fountain, the blinding white light, so much like the glittering sun, twinkles like diamonds, like stars in shimmering arabesques; here, varicolored pyramids of light formed by red, green, yellow, blue and white lanterns glitter and gleam. On the broad ways and narrow paths, people will crowd to see and be seen, and everywhere there is music, rejoiceful music!

The Vaudeville Theatre in Olympic Park is without equal. It has seats for 4,000 people where all are protected under a waterproof roof. The colossal stage is 100 feet wide from one wall to the other, with a depth of 40 feet. Only the best of specialized stages is

good enough for Olympic Park! Here, productions shall be no mere appendage as is customarily the case in other summer places; rather, a first-class vaudeville program will grace this new temple of the tenth muse. Presentations in which only stars of the American and European artistic world are featured will find a home in this new, mammoth theatre every afternoon and evening.

A person must eat—it makes no difference where he is—and especially is this so when pangs of hunger pinch the stomach. In order to put to rights the inner man, the 150-foot-long dining hall located under the dance pavilion has been joined by a two-story food pavilion newly built for your pleasure. Here one can sit on the second story of this restaurant as if on a roof garden. The press of mankind will pass before you—the ballroom with its dancing young people; the new carousel constructed at a cost of $25,000; and, in the background, the cars of the figure-8 toboggan slide rushing past.

The menu boasts of over 300 different items. The kitchen is supervised by Rudolphe Lange, chef for many years at the Hotel Victoria, who is supported by four competent cooks. A bakery on the premises makes it possible to offer guests fresh cake and tortes for their pleasure at all hours.

The restaurant's popular prices will enable everyone to have their meals at Olympic Park. And when a woman accompanied by her children or friends comes during the afternoon for fresh-brewed coffee and cake baked on the premises, she will not have to hurry home to cook for her husband. No! He can join her after work to enjoy a better and cheaper supper in a setting under God's heaven, on the veranda of the Olympic Park restaurant.

Olympic Park will not be a Coney Island, but rather a place for pleasant family excursions. The owners have willingly foregone large amounts of money by refusing to allow games of chance which do nothing more than empty the public's pockets. Such games, which generally attract mostly young people at other amusement parks, are banned at Olympic Park. Also denied entrance are gypsies and soothsayers with their double-tongued art. Women and children can stroll through Olympic Park at any time without fear, assured of safety by police protection provided by the management. All unsavory elements will

be excluded.

Among other attractions are a scenic electrical illusion, "The Fall of Port Arthur," which is highly educational for young and old alike. The park's menagerie has been improved with the addition of new animals and a beautiful variety of birds.

Before the park closes for the evening, rocket displays signal the beginning of the fireworks. The pyrotechnics at Olympic Park were most popular last year. Patrons already know that the fireworks, using the highest grade American powder, are all that the eye can desire. The multi-colored display, the glittering light, are an enchantment for everyone.

Der Erzähler
May 21, 1905

A Contented Audience

Rain marred the pleasures of the various amusement parks in this neighborhood one night recently, and there was a lot of other trouble at Olympic Park. Mr. Wevers, the manager, was kept on the jump for two hours, and when he emerged from the wreck his collar was wilted, but his happy disposition was unchanged. The rain was bad enough to spoil any one's temper, but Mr. Wevers simply shrugged his shoulders and declared that rain was to be expected. Shortly after 8 o'clock, however, just as the musicians were preparing to play the overture for the "Pirates of Penzance" all the lights went out. There was absolute darkness. Never has there been gathered together so patient an audience as that crowd that sat there in the total blackness of a rainy night, waiting for the light. The trouble couldn't be located and Hans Wevers managed to get some candles from somewhere, and these he put near the orchestra. And so, by candlelight and memory, the musicians played a number of popular selections, which the audience sang with great effect, no one being afraid to sing right out loud because no one could see anybody else. Then a chorus came from out of the inky darkness, where the stage ought to be, and a few songs by professional talent cheered the waiters. For two long hours Hans Wevers managed to keep that audience contented, and then he announced that ticket money would be refunded. No sooner had the little audience dispersed than the lights went up.

The Amusement News
July 1906

Opening of Olympic Park

Music lovers and amusement seekers in this city and neighboring communities, who found pleasing entertainment in the operatic performances given in Olympic Park . . . during the past two summers, and other agreeable pastimes in that admirably conducted resort, will welcome the announcement that Manager Schmidt will inaugurate the regular summer season there to-day. The scheme of entertainment arranged by him undoubtedly will make the Olympic even more attractive than formerly. A large force of workmen has been employed during the past few months in such ways as will increase accommodations for visitors, add to the comforts previously provided, make the spacious grove and grounds more beautiful, and afford facilities for a greater variety of entertainment than previously invited attention.

Much attention has been bestowed on the theatre, the largest and best equipped playhouse in any summer park in this section, which is so constructed that it combines the advantages of an open air theatre and an enclosed auditorium wherein performance can be given without patrons being incommoded by sudden changes from dry to wet weather. Entertainment therein during the coming season will be provided by the Olympic Park Opera Company, which will make its first appearance Sunday night . . . .

It is the intention of the management to present musical comedies of the modern sort as well as the more popular of the comic operas in which the music is as important as the humorous scheme . . . .

The musical offerings will not be the only means of diversion afforded by the management. Beginning to-day an entertainment styled "A Society Circus" will be a feature of the season's attractions and will be given in a special arena constructed for it. The program will comprise performances by Bristol's trained ponies, educated horse and kicking mule and several aerial acts by expert gymnasts and acrobats. For the opening week Manager Schmidt also has engaged the services of Arthur Holden, the noted high diver, who also will perform twice daily his daring and perilous feat of looping the loop. Archie Griffin, the famous aeronaut, also will be a member of the entertaining forces at the park and will make two balloon ascensions daily.

The large dancing pavilion, whose fine floor makes it particularly inviting to dancers, has been put in excellent condition and with an excellent orchestra will be in readiness for all who wish to enjoy that pastime there to-day. The restaurant, which became so popular with many patrons of the park during the past two seasons owing to the quality of the food and the appetizing manner in which it was served, again will be conducted in the way that built up its reputation and made it such an inviting place for diners summer afternoons and evenings.

Newark Sunday News
May 25, 1907

Horse Falls in Race at Olympic

Patrons of the race meet at Olympic Park, yesterday afternoon, were treated to a bit of excitement not on the card when, in the first heat of the third race, Admorell, driven by Cliff Woodruff, fell while rounding the back stretch, and before Dr. Elias Bodenweiser, owner and driver of Hamlet, who was following close behind, could check his horse, he ran over the fallen animal. The spectators lost interest in the heat because of the accident, which occurred in full view of the grandstand, but upon learning that neither horse nor driver had been injured settled back to enjoy the rest of the racing. It was said that Admorell was crowded

while rounding the turn. The horse went down headfirst and shot the driver from his seat as if he was thrown from a catapult. Woodruff landed on his feet several yards away. Admorell's knees were cut and he was withdrawn from the race.

Syron, who drove The Sultan in the 2.27 trot, was found guilty of holding the horse back in the third heat and was fined $10 and suspended for 90 days. Syron tried to have the officials give him a hearing, but they refused to re-open the case. Syron could easily have beaten Highland Laddy in this heat, it was said, but at the three-quarter mark, pulled his horse in. He was jeered for his action by the crowd as the horses came around in front of the judges' stand.

The largest crowd of the year turned out to witness the races, more than 4,000 persons looking on while an excellent card was gone through.

Newark Evening News
Sept. 7, 1909

Motorcyclist Margaret Gould Issues Challenge

The motorcycle racing fever is spreading rapidly throughout Newark and vicinity. Margaret Gould, the female baseball pitcher, has taken up the sport and has developed into a speed artist of no mean ability. She has a high power twin cylinder machine, and is out with a challenge to meet any woman motorcyclist in a match race. She has been a spectator at the Sunday afternoon race meets held at Olympic Park and has tried out the track.

There are many women motorcyclists in this city and vicinity, but they are not devoted to racing, and a match between two devotees of the sport would be decidedly interesting. Under the rules of the Federation of Motorcyclists, woman riders are not permitted to compete in races with men. Consequently such a match would have to be a special affair.

Newark Evening News
Oct. 1, 1910

61

Good News for Mothers and Children

Last year the "Freie Zeitung" gave away thousands of free season tickets to Olympic Park, though one might have hoped that requests for them would have been more numerous. The fact is that a good portion of our German mothers are slaves to their housework from which they enjoy little diversion. Monday, Wednesday and every day of the week brings its routine work and many women accordingly believe they have no time for a little enjoyment. But they are wrong.

No, mothers, do not be so hard on yourselves. Think, life is short, and do not pass up the opportunity to take advantage of a break. These free season tickets will put you in a position to enjoy at least one or more afternoons of the week in the cool, shady surroundings of Olympic Park. The beautiful band music, the vaudeville acts and the other amusements will cost you no more than 10 cents. Take your sewing along with you when you go to the park.

Think of the great joy and the colossal relaxation you can derive with your children from the season tickets. A great amusement park, open for you on several days of the week during the entire summer (with the exception of Sundays and Fridays) means dollars' worth of healthful recreation for the children and for the mothers. Also, mothers, if you cannot go yourself every week, let the little ones go. They will be much better off there than on the hot, dusty streets or in steamy rooms. Give them the admission tickets and enough food to wile away the whole day in the park. If you think they cannot find their own way to the park, let them go with playmates.

N.J. *Freie Zeitung*
1911

Car Overturns, One Burns in Exciting Contests

Thrills galore were dished up to the automobile race enthusiasts last Saturday afternoon and night at the meet held at Olympic Park. The majority of these came at night. The one which sent a shudder through the crowd was the burning of a Chalmers Blue Streak, from which Bill Brown, the driver, had a narrow escape from serious injury. Another car, driven by Captain Kennedy, threw a wheel during the running of the 50-mile race at night and only skillful handling prevented it from turning turtle. The thrill in the matinee session was furnished by Ben Gotof. The Flying Dutchman drove his car through a fence and sustained a fractured collar bone.

The burning of the car occurred on the back stretch after the finish of the free-for-all at three miles. A flame shot high in the air and Brown ran his car around to the center of the turn, heading into the home stretch. There he shut off the power and jumped from the blazing machine. No sooner had he cleared when both the gasoline and acetylene tanks exploded. The flames soon mounted high in the air and, although efforts were made to put out the blaze, they were unsuccessful. The car was totally destroyed.

In trying to avoid a car in front of him, which started to skid as a result of blowing a tire, Ben Gotof shot off the track on the first turn. His car turned turtle and Gotof slid along the ground for a distance of about 20 feet.

Newark *Evening News*
July 26, 1915

Olympic Park Making Ready for Decoration Day

Olympic Park is practically ready now, but the management is disposed to break all records for beauty of scene, for comfort throughout the entire 24 acres, and for variety of entertainment —to which ends: floral displays in all directions, renovation of buildings and protection of paths, and the engagement of Professor Vintcenz's Military Band and sundry selected novelty artists, including "Herera, the man up the Pole." Later—early in July—the Aborn Opera Company inaugurate their eleventh season at this resort, in- cluding in a comprehensive program of popular musical productions being "The Firefly," "The Prince of Pilsen," "The Red Mill," "Robin Hood," "The Mikado," "Gypsy Love," and "The Blue Paradise." If only for the opportunity of dancing in one of the largest and finest dance halls in the country, there should be thousands taking the car to Olympic Park—either their own car (for which there is adequate parking space) or the trolley (which lands them at the entrance gates within 25 minutes' ride from the centre of the city). The half mile race track, the opera house, the dance hall, the diversity of side shows, the performance on the open-air stage, the music, the splendid conveniences for dining and banqueting at reasonable prices, the healthful location, the pleasing "get-up" of the grounds, and the nominal charge for admission, and above all, the care taken to exclude any objectionable element—these factors combine to make Olympic Park the ideal summer retreat for the family—a place where an entire day may be spent to mental and physical advantage.

Maplewood *Home News*
May 11, 1917

Police Called to Stop Bessie's Monkey Shines

Special policemen on the Olympic Park staff are planning to invite their brothers-in-arms of the Newark police force, who last week acquired big game hunting practice by capturing nine wild goats in the Ironbound section, to demonstrate their knowledge in effecting the capture of Bessie.

Bessie is an agile, brown monkey that escaped Friday from one of the acts at the park and has been at large —very much at large—since then. Her owner, William Hill, had to take his trained animal act to New York Saturday, where he was under contract, but Bessie remained behind.

Otto Kessler, an Irvington special policeman and chief of the park staff, was busy yesterday forenoon denying rumors that a monkey was loose when a chorus of yells and shrieks from the greenhouse interrupted him. The crash of splintering glass hastened his steps and, as he approached the structure, Bessie skipped through a hole in the roof and scampered over the automobile parking space to vanish in a grove of trees.

Nicholas Giuliano, one of the parking concessionaires, ruefully explained that the monkey had just stolen a basket of lunch from someone's parked automobile as he came in sight, that he had given chase to Bessie and she, seeking refuge in the greenhouse, had said it with flowers to him by hurling potted plants at him and at the glass walls and roof of the structure.

Chief Kessler, rather discountenanced by this denial of his denial that a monkey was frolicking around loose, joined forces with two other special policemen, but the monkey had concealed herself in the foliage. Occasionally throughout the day she could be seen frolicking among the parked automobiles committing such pranks as stealing straw hats and piling them in one automobile. At the slightest sign of pursuit she vanished.

When she escaped Friday night, Bessie was pursued to a store room where electric wires and bulbs are kept. She laid down a well-directed barrage of colored electric light bulbs which kept the police at bay and then skipped through an open window and into some trees.

Her whereabouts was discovered Saturday morning when pandemonium broke loose in a nearby hencoop, where Bessie was discovered plucking the feathers from a prize fowl. Except for raids on concessionaires' stands where fruit is displayed and the theft of a Panama hat from a volunteer huntsman, Bessie kept pretty much to herself the remainder of the day.

Policeman William Brehme's greatest ire was aroused when, after pursuing the animal for two days, he found Bessie perched on the roof of his automobile when he went off duty last night.

Newark *Evening News*
July 21, 1924

Not Just Another Amusement Park

Before entering Olympic Park, the visitor is impressed with the conviction that he has come upon something besides just another amusement park. There is probably no park in the country laid out in just the manner you will find here.

After coming through the charming entrance of stucco and the Olympic legend of "Smile" at the top of the arch, one cannot be quite sure that he is in an amusement park. This is exactly the way Henry A. Guenther, owner and director of the park, wishes you to feel. He wishes to convey no impression whatever that would sow in your mind the suspicion that this is a commercial enterprise and that you are here to spend money.

What Mr. Guenther wishes you to realize, and he is certainly successful at it, is that here, first and foremost, is a place for you to enjoy yourself. So, when you have entered the main gate, you see no attractions and neither do you hear barkers or the roar of mechanical rides. Instead you look upon a charming, shady and cool vista of trees and flowers in the center of which is an inviting picnic grove. And there are comfortable benches galore.

The main walkways at Olympic are concrete. The roads are cinders. The concrete, for the most part, is shaded so that it does not become hot under foot . . . .

The first building you come upon is the administration building. It is, in fact, a cottage and a very picturesque one. You arrive at it after you have passed through the gate (it is a 10-cent gate to all over 10 years of age) and also after you have passed the old cafe beside the entrance.

This cafe, by the way, can bear a little description because there is probably not another like it in any other amusement park in these high and dry days. It has been left just about as it was in the days when a beer meant something besides a stomach wash. Inside you will find a mahogany bar, and a little further on is what used to be known as "the back room." This part can also be entered through a "family entrance" on the side.

All kinds of soft drinks are sold here, including "near-beer," and it is a popular place. For many Jerseyites, if they are to drink anything at all, prefer the old time cafe atmosphere. And that is just the reason why Mr. Guenther, who knows his people, has left it there.

The administration building or cottage, besides housing its various offices of executives, also houses the Victor Orthophonic and one loudspeaker.

The other loudspeaker is at the pool.

On the right we have a line of buildings leading along the edge of the grove. They include a "Mother's Rest Room" and a very pretty wash room building. Between these two is a free kiddies playground with swings, slides, etc. Like everything in this part of the park they are all well shaded.

One thing we must not forget is the color scheme of Olympic and its sign system. The color scheme is always the same—green and white. Green for restfulness, white for cleanliness. And the sign system consists of neat white and green swinging boards which, for the most part, are hung from shade trees. Nothing blares at you, not even the signs nor the loudspeaker, which is kept in control at all times.

To the left across the grove we have the ballroom, a two-story structure with the dance floor above and refreshment stands beneath. This ballroom is one of the great successes of Olympic Park.

In the center of the grove is the band stand. At the inner end of the grove we come upon, hidden among the trees, refreshment booths and a wild animal show. On the right, beside the restaurant, refreshment stands and the new Pretzel ride and games, is, at the end of the walk, the Custer ride. You never saw a Custer ride exactly like this because, just within the entrance, there is a cage full of Rhesus monkeys. They are there as an added attraction for the ride.

On the crosswalk leading to the left there now protrudes the mammoth and grotesque Bluebeard Castle front. This is always a lively place, for spectators love to watch the girls as they come out on the little balconies, etc., and encounter the blow valves.

Continuing to the left we come upon the Ferris Wheel, the Whip and the Dodgem. At this point we encounter the walk that runs down the left side of the grove and here are located game booths, Jack Rabbit coaster, Old Mill, Merry-Go-Round and Penny Arcade. At this point is located the ramp which leads down onto the lower level of the park, for Olympic is built on two levels separated by a retaining wall.

Before we go down the ramp let's proceed down toward the free act stage located at the end of the park among a beautiful cluster of shade trees. The trees are particularly cool-looking here because the entire end of the park is bounded by . . . [a small brook] which chortles along between grassy banks. This part of the park has been left to its natural beauty.

Before we reach the large open space in which the audience watches the acts we come to what is probably the oldest miniature golf course in any amusement park. In fact, this golf course was installed long before the craze of last year—it is at least four years old, to be exact.

Now we turn left to go down the ramp and here we see the big pool and the big cluster of rides and amusements.

In a square at one end of the pool are laid out the following attractions: Pony Ride, Chair-O-Plane, Lindy Loop, Tilt-A-Whirl, Circle Swing, Dip-Lo-Do-Cus, Paradise, Wax Show, 1001 Troubles, Hey Day, the new Cuddle Up, Bug, Leaping Lena, new Flight Tutor, Archery Court, Upside Down House, Illusion Show, etc.

The pool, being such a large one, takes up most of this end of the park and beyond it is Kiddieland with its grotesque fence and colored rides.

Amusement Park Management
August 1931

New Endurance Test Starts on Dance Floor Sunday

Sunday night will bring to the Olympic Park Dance Marathon contestants an entirely new grueling test of endurance in the form of a two-hour sprint that will take every effort of these kids to abide by the rigid rules set before them by the impartial judges. Never before in the history of dance marathons has such a test of human endurance been inflicted upon the contestants after so many hours of hard nerve wracking continual motion. There will be two groups of dancers, each team chained together and they will be expected to lap 120 times around the dance floor during the Sprint Test in order to remain in the contest. Owing to the size of this great ballroom, it will tax every bit of energy that remains in these kids in order for them to make this number of laps; it

will mean that they will have to go at a terrific speed and that they will be under the most severe kind of arm strain. They will be allowed five minutes hospital treatment out of each half hour, but they will not have time to leave the floor. The doctors, nurses and trainers will be placed on the ballroom floor with the hospital equipment and the kids will receive first aid treatment in full view of the audience. It is not expected that many of these youngsters will be able to make the grade and that is not to be wondered at, for by the time this hard Sprint Grind starts they will have completed their 1,969th hour.

It does not seem possible that they can carry on under these grinds which so rapidly follow on another and under the strict rules that are now enforced every minute of the day and night. It is only because of the pluck of our group of kids that this marathon has not already ended.

Olympic Park *Marathon News*
Dec. 17, 1932

When You Don't Feel Like Skating

When our skaters are too tired to skate or the weather is too warm, where do they usually go? Nine out of 10 times, you'll find them in the park enjoying the rides or at the stands. The roller coaster is a thrilling ride many skaters go on as soon as they leave the rink after evening and matinee sessions. Rides such as the Octopus and the Leapin' Lena give riders a good tossing around and make them yell for more. Ducking the negro at the Afri-dip provides the ball throwers an opportunity to show the accuracy of their mighty arms. A ride through the Haunted Castle will give you chills and thrills plus a chance to be alone with that certain someone. Our big brawny he-men can strut their prowess by trying to ring the bell on the High Striker. For the tots, the park offers an entertaining time in Kiddie Land.

Spend the day at the stands trying your luck. Poker Fascination gives the poker players a chance to show the luck and skill they lack at other times. Hoopla tests your ability to put a hoop about a desired object, offering a prize

whether the tosser wins or losses. Casey's Penny Palace and the Penny Tossing game gives a chance to put your spare pennies to good use for worthwhile prizes. Cigarette smokers can win a few extra packages at the Cigarette Game and fishermen down on their luck can find consolation at the Fish Pond. Bowlers are put at ease at the Miniature Bowling Alleys and the ladies can try their luck at winning a few pairs of good silk stockings at the stocking concession. Let Professor "Guess Your Age" have a try at your age; become a second "Robin Hood" at Archery; knock the midget serenaders over the fence at the Giant Cat Game; or ride the Scoota Boats in preparation for your summer vacation. For a thrill, ride the Tumble Bug and the Auto Speedway. Everyone is invited to win radios, lamps or groceries at Shuffle Score, the Meat Stand, the Dice Game or Spill the Milk. If you think you don't show your weight, why not let the weight guesser have a try? Maybe you'll win a prize for being able to hide your secret.

For your pleasure and convenience, whenever you get hungry or thirsty the park has numerous food and drink concessions run by Caffrey and Giuliano at which that empty or dry feeling can be satisfied. If you would rather have a dip or two of refreshing ice cream or custard, the Frozen Custard stand can fill that order to a tee. Cones are a nickel. Giant cones are a mere dime.

For those hot summer days when Ol' Sol makes skating a bit too warm, Olympic has the finest swimming pool in the East. Here you'll find diving boards of various heights, plenty of shallow water for non-swimmers, and lots of room for those who can. The pool also has a fine, large natural sand beach where many spend enjoyable hours. Admission is 50¢, children under 12, 28¢. Night bathing after 6p.m. is also 28¢. Ladies have the free use of hair dryers.

So don't forget, skaters, when you are hot and want to cool off, go to the swimming pool. When you want to spend an evening that's different, go out in the park and join the hundreds of others who are enjoying the various amusements of Olympic Park. And don't forget the big free circus twice daily.

All in all, there are plenty of ways of enjoying yourselves when you don't feel like skating right here in Olympic Park. If the day is too weary to do anything, the Park also has a very good picnic grove, so pack up a good lunch and come over. The grove is situated in a desirable spot with many benches and tables placed under large trees that provide ample shade on the hottest days. Close by to the grove you will find our bar where you will be able to get that delicious cold glass of beer or soft drink to go with your sandwiches.

Olympic Park Press Release
Summer, 1941

Meet Eddie Baatz

"Before the next number, I would like to wish a Happy Birthday to—" Sound familiar? Sure it does! Eddie chants it almost every night to someone. Usually he announces the age, too, making certain, of course, that he either makes them five years older or younger than they really are. The sillier it sounds, the happier he is!!

Have you ever been in the organ room? If you haven't, take heed to the warning and "DO NOT ENTER!" From the moment you enter until you leave, you'll be plagued with corny jokes and surprising wise-cracks. But you have to admit, Baatzie's got a sense of humor that could make "dead pan" himself have hysterics.

Good old Eddie is one that isn't forgotten, not even by the long-gone servicemen. Every letter so far received has said "Remember me to Eddie Baatz." Just that quotation is enough to make him happy and go on plugging for War Bonds and Stamps.

No matter who you are, if you know Eddie you're in for some sort of teasing about something. He gets around, and if he can't find anything to tease you about, he just makes something up. He plays songs that have special meanings for certain people and gets such a kick out of what he's doing that you just can't get sore at him. Look at him pitifully to make him stop, then you really get it—"it" being the most devilish boyish grin you ever did see. And the minute he knows you're suffering, you are licked!!!

But never let it be said that Eddie isn't respected and extremely well liked by everyone who knows him, especially for his sense of humor, generosity and infectious smile.

Well, kids, I hope you know the little man in the glass case a little better 'cause he's the guy that puts the "jitterbug" in you with his super solid jive. He's the boy who makes the music go 'round and 'round and come out mighty sweet to put you in just the right mood to kiss and make-up.

We'll say hello to him for all you guys and gobs in service too. I hope you enjoyed meeting Eddie (Cupid) Baatz.

Dog House
July 1945

Eyes Reveal Age Claims Showman at Olympic Park

Camouflage your eyes, foreheads and necks, gals, if you would shield your age!

That is the sage advice of Frank Baker, who lives handsomely by guessing the ages of old, young and indeterminate, at Olympic Park. Baker has learned that his surmises are 85 per cent correct, and he adds that a third of those who say he did not guess within two years "just don't admit the true facts."

The eyes, Baker has found, are peculiarly telltale in their expressions. Foreheads are the next clue and the flabbiness of necks provides the clinching diagnosis. Baker discounts greying hair, posture and similar physical characteristics as potentials in any age.

The patent office in Washington balked him when he sought to patent his trade—rebuffing him with the assertion that his show is a game of chance. After 13 years at it, commented Baker, he knows it is only skill, patience, and tact.

Union Register
August 4, 1949

Skin Diver Sets Mark

Ernest J. "Red" Stevens, 22-year-old skin diver from Kearny, yesterday broke the world record for underwater endurance at Olympic Park swimming pool. Stevens stayed submerged 31 hours and 10 minutes to beat the record of 30 hours and 9 minutes set Friday by a St. Louis lifeguard.

Stevens' 19-year-old wife was among the thousands of onlookers who cheered him when Stevens emerged from the water at 3:23p.m. yesterday. He hugged his wife and said, "Boy, I feel wet."

His co-workers started to pull Stevens from the water Saturday afternoon during an electrical storm but the diver elected to remain underwater.

The Kearny diver was fed hot tea, soup, coffee and other liquids from a plastic bag. He passed the time reading paperback novels, playing cards with fellow divers and, when the cards began to float away, by playing checkers.

The other divers also watched his condition and when he passed the previous world mark, they decided not to let him stay down until 7p.m. as originally planned. Stevens had gone entirely without sleep and fatigue was beginning to show when he came out of the water. He was taken to a first aid room where a doctor said his condition was "generally good." Stevens said he will not try again until someone beats his record.

Stevens wore a black rubber suit that covered his entire body. His aqua lung changes were made at 45 to 60 minute intervals. A bench was provided at one end of the pool for Stevens and he walked about on the bottom of the pool to keep his circulation going.

Newark Evening News
July 14, 1958

Finds New Hobby in Pool Sand

Charles Chadwyke of East Orange idly scraped the sand at the Olympic Park pool recently and found a new hobby—sand sculpturing.

Bored with basking in the sun, Chadwyke began shaping the sand surrounding him into people, animals and cartoon characters and crowds began to gather around with suggestions for other subjects. Now he's so busy filling requests he doesn't have time to be bored.

Most of the requests Chadwyke gets come from children who want to see their favorite comic or TV character shaped in sand. So far he has been able to live up to their demands.

Among the favorites created by Chadwyke is a six-foot-tall pharoah, creeping commandos armed with rifles, dinosaurs and Indian chiefs. He has also made busts of Sen. John Kennedy and Vice President Richard M. Nixon.

Chadwyke, who has been drawing most of his life, begins planning his sculptures while taking the bus to the park. His only tools are a spatula, his hands and a bucket of water to fuse the sand.

A completed piece will take anywhere from 15 minutes to an hour or more, depending upon the subject. It takes longer to make people than animals, he said. "The hardest part is piling the sand. It might take an hour and a half, depending on the height of the subject."

Like a true artist, Chadwyke hates to leave his creations, "because I know they're going to be destroyed." They last about three days if no one breaks them, according to Chadwyke.

Newark *Evening News*
August 21, 1960

Essex Jet Set

The big chrome and green bus screeched to a stop on the long-unused trolley tracks still embedded in the cement. It disgorged a bunch of happy city kids who scrambled for the park entrance. They plucked their quarters down at the turnstile, hastened past the trick mirrors and ran for something called "The Jet."

An older fellow, who remembers when The Jet was just called the "Roller Coaster" and didn't go so fast, pushed his coin through to a pleasant grey-haired lady.

When he entered the park he made a hasty right turn after looking in one of those mirrors that makes you look like 300 pounds. He walked to an unpretentious two-story wood building tucked in a corner of the park next to the swings.

From that vantage point, two brothers, Robert and Henry Guenther Jr., run Olympic Park and its 40 acres of amusements. Outside, the kids were screaming with delighted "fright" on The Jet. They were so "scared" of the ride that Guenther had to soup it up in 1951 because "Kids today demand more thrills."

That's the story all over the park. A boy 20 years ago would hop on a putt-putt motorboat to get kicks. Now, he's got the Flying Saucer, a car that floats on air.

Or there's the Wild Mouse, a miniature roller coaster with a bite. A sweet-looking 13-year-old girl wearing the expression of a jet pilot as she rode that thing screamed, "I think I left my stomach up there at the first turn."

"Yeh," giggled her companion. "Let's go on again."

Up the road is the Cuddle Up, swirling little cars that shake you up until the contents of your stomach turns to buttermilk. Right next to it is that nostalgic old amusement attraction which has lost a little of its luster in the race for speed—the merry go round.

"The teenagers used to like the merry go round, but it doesn't mean much to them anymore. It's popular for the small kids." Guenther said.

Olympic's merry go round . . . is still, in the showman's word, the "largest in the country," although the big swimming pool is now "one of the biggest, not the biggest any more."

Some of the kids who live a short bicycle ride away from the park in Irvington, Maplewood or Union have found new horizons.

The roller coaster or the putt-putts don't mean so much to a suburban teenager who has his own car by the time he graduates from high school. He has new frontiers—the shore, the lakes and New York City.

But although the kid who grows up here in the shadow of the coaster may look elsewhere, a crowd of boys and girls who a generation ago wouldn't have had the means or method to get to Olympic, are now making the pilgrimage.

"We get boys coming up from New Brunswick, for example. Now that they have cars they can do that," Guenther said. According to Guenther, 30,000 attended the park on Memorial Day.

Newark *Evening News*
June 8, 1964

Thrills, Chills in Olympic Park

A six-minute amusement park ride stretched into 2½ hours last night and —depending on your age—was either a "nightmare" or a "ball."

At Olympic Park in Irvington there's a ride called The Skyline. Modeled after a ski-tow, the ride carries its passengers for 1,000 feet out and back again on a tour of the park and rises 35 feet off the ground.

At 7:40, a cable slipped off its wheel and the ride stopped. With it stopped some 30 passengers.

Some, near the entrance to the ride, got off immediately. Others were able to get off via 35-foot fire ladders set against the cables. But seven riders near the turn-around of the ride had to sit in the narrow, three-passenger seats while the cable was replaced and their chairs hand-cranked down to a waiting aerial ladder manned by members of the fire department.

Once off the ride, reactions were mixed. Mrs. Anthony Nufrio of Irvington said, "I just sat and prayed." But her son, Anthony Jr., said, "It was scary but sort of fun."

Typically, the adults were frightened. "The only thing I could think about was the concrete sidewalk 30 feet below." said Joseph Stracuzzi Sr. of Linden.

The exception was Anthony Tortoriello of Newark who was stranded for two hours with his two children, Jo Ann, 12, and Vincent, 10. "We weren't too scared," he said, "and we were able to get a great bird's eye view of the circus and the park."

Newark *Evening News*
July 29, 1965

8

THE GOLDEN AGE

The Twenties were the golden age of the amusement park business. Never had so many Americans crowded through the turnstiles in search of excitement, all willing victims of a craze for outdoor amusement that began after the Great War and raged unabated until the Depression dimmed the nation's exuberance. Before World War I, many Americans frowned on amusement parks as hangouts for rowdies, drunks or foreigners. All of that changed as the nation returned to its peculiar postwar version of "normalcy." New parks sprang up everywhere. Established ones shed their old images, installing rides that featured greater speed and the illusion of danger. Park owners and ride designers cudgeled their brains for new ways to satisfy the millions of patrons who boarded the trolley or family Model T for a day-long outing at their local amusement park.

Olympic's 1920 season was the last in the Schmidt tradition. When the park reopened in May 1921, it had been converted, as the local paper put it, "into a veritable funland of the kind known at Coney Island as Steeplechase Park."

"Entering through the Palace Sanitarium, the visitor at once experiences a number of surprises, and therefore can spend hours on the barrel chain, the social mixer, the haunted castle, the alpine slide, in the melting pot, in the revolving barrel, on the wiggle-woggle, in the squeezer, etc. One inclusive charge entitles [one] to stay the whole day."

"Another big park feature is Weir's jungle of trained and performing tigers, lions, bears, leopards, monkeys, birds, and other animals—an entire performance inside a finely appointed tent. The large variety of side shows at Olympic Park includes the old mill, the human tangle, carousel, the whip, caverns, aeroplane, frolic, ferris wheel and roller-coaster. The beautiful mirrored dance hall at Olympic Park where dancing has been held this season on Saturday nights only is now to be open every night. On Sundays concerts are given at Olympic Park by Charles Quenthor's Band, both afternoon and evening. A new open-air stage has been built at the Olympic Park grounds, and on this there will be two performances daily by Hocum's Circus, introducing a full complement of gymnasts, acrobats, equestrians, equilebrists, performing mules, educated dogs, unridable mules and clowns."

Henry Guenther spent thousands transforming Olympic into a non-alcoholic amusement park of the kind made famous by Coney Island, a format that was to endure until the gates closed 44 years later. The new Olympic Park was an instant success. Attendance grew rapidly until it reached a peak of more than one million in 1930, the park's best year. Centerpiece of the park was the Palace of Fun, formerly the opera house, which the C.S. Rose Co. of Baltimore converted into a funhouse at a cost of $50,000. The opening of the pool in 1923 and the installation of a new carousel in 1929 were among the highlights of a successful and highly-profitable

The opera house emerged as the "Palace of 25 Attractions" for the 1921 season, from a postcard. See page 79 for an interior view of Olympic's own version of the Steeplechase.

decade that saw Olympic Park develop into one of the nation's premier parks.

One of the few traditions of the Schmidt era Guenther retained was the free vaudeville performances given afternoon and evening on a stage erected at the rear of the park near Lightning Brook. "The stage is a large open air platform and in its rear is a band shell in which the band plays while the acts are on," wrote one observer. "The program is changed weekly, all professional acts being booked through Wirth & Hamid. One of the interesting things about the free acts at Olympic is that patrons are perfectly willing to stand up to see the performance. There are no seats. A large grassy space in front of the stage is used and here the people stand and see a short but interesting program with no complaint whatever about the discomfort of standing. Although there are goodly and appreciative crowds watching the program, in the afternoons and evenings, it is at night that the largest crowds turn out for them." The program, auditioned, booked and arranged by Guenther himself, lasted no more than 20 to 25 minutes. "In this way," added the writer, "although the patrons are given something really worthwhile

for their 10 cent gate admission, they are not tied up for any length of time." Animal acts, said Guenther, drew the best: "It does not matter much what kind of an animal act it is either. They can be wild animals or tame ones, big ones or small ones, they do better here than anything else we can get, except children's revues." Major Al Criqui, the park's well-known major-domo, a former professional midget who officiated at Olympic Park for more than a decade, announced the shows.

While animal acts were the park's mainstay, Guenther booked a variety of performers. "Olympic Park patrons will have an opportunity next week of witnessing one of the finest spectacles ever presented to the public when Bill Richie's great water show will appear," announced the park with its usual modesty. "The act includes a splendid array of divinely beautiful naiads whose supple, sylph-like forms flash through the air with an easy grace in a series of trick, fancy and somersaulting dives. The concluding and most thrilling feature of this sterling act is offered by the greatest of all high divers, Captain Jack Hoover, who [from] atop a small platform on a ladder which towers into the very clouds, 115 feet above the water

68

Henry A. Guenther

level, turns a complete somersault in the air, alighting in a small tank that is a veritable seething cauldron of fire." A year later, in August 1929, The Great Wilno, billed as the "human projectile," appeared direct from Germany. "[C]onsidered one of the greatest gasp-producing supersensations of the age, Wilno will be shot out of a giant Howitzer twice daily. He will be tossed 40 feet into the air and thence for a distance of 150 feet into a net unscathed." Wilno, added Olympic Park publicity manager Frank J. McTague, "literally flirts with death every time he performs the feat." More typical of the vaudeville acts seen in the Twenties were Sofie and Niles Hellkvist, "an accomplished duo of athletes" who presented an array of acrobatic and trick diving during the week of June 1, 1928, and the Kanzazana Japs, a "quintet of clever Japanese masters" whose August 1928 routine included juggling, foot posturing, barrel kicking "and acrobatic risky work." Headliners during mid-July 1929 were the Tom Davies Trio, three motorcyclists who "careen madly around a 'tea-cup' track performing various hair-raising feats, the climax being reached when the riders race recklessly around the track, while it is being raised in mid-air, during which the least slip would mean instantaneous death to the riders."

Daylong outings sponsored by clubs, unions and business firms were popular during the Twenties,

many drawing huge crowds. In addition to the usual rides and amusements available at the park, the outings featured foot races, baseball games, tugs of war, dancing and band concerts. On August 26, 1922, the H.G. McCully chapter of the Telephone Pioneers of America held its first annual meeting at the Park. Some 3,000 telephone people and their families attended. For the convenience of mothers with small children, the park offered a special "baby-pavilion" equipped with trained nurses, toys and kiddie rides. The Telephone Pioneers held their annual outings at the park for five consecutive years. Other groups enjoying the park's facilities were the Prudential Athletic Assn., the New Jersey Exempt Firemen's Assn., the P.B.A., the Kiwanis and the Boy Scouts. One of the biggest crowds of the decade filled the park in August 1929 when the Hyatt Roller Bearing Co. held its annual field day and family reunion. An estimated 5,000 people attended.

Guenther encouraged use of the park's facilities by charitable organizations. In 1921, a Hoover Dinner raised funds to aid starving children in war-torn Europe. A $2.50 ticket entitled the bearer to a "dinner" of shredded wheat and skimmed milk. Forty thousand visitors packed into Olympic Park for an industrial and commercial exhibition in the spring of 1925. "The resourcefulness displayed in devising advertising schemes was certainly interesting," mar-

The park's gold elephant carried a basket full of delighted children.

The Midway, from the ramp, 1923. From left, the Rambler, Aeroplane Swing and Diplodocus, a small roller coaster.

During the Twenties and Thirties circus viewers had to stand. Seats were not provided because it was thought patrons would linger too long at the free attraction.

The Ice Cream Parlor was only one of Olympic's many waist-widening attractions, from a postcard, c. 1920.

The picnic grove was cool even on the hottest day, thanks to the many large trees.

veled the local paper. "Most visitors. . .probably remember meeting a highly snobbish-looking male individual, a monocle perched over an eye and wearing a top hat of doubtful vintage. That was supposed to be the 'man who never smiles,' and he was stalking around to advertise the superior quality of gas ranges, radiators and heaters for which Maier-Rich & Co. are distributors. The concern offered a $25 prize to any one who could make him smile. A woman found a way on Tuesday evening. She smacked him on the cheek and got a water heater for her ordeal."

A Boy's Hobby Show and Achievement Exposition in 1927, a gymnastic exhibition by the National Turnverein in 1928, and annual Boy Scout, Junior Order, Holy Name and Elks Days were popular.

Local political figures booked their most important events at Olympic Park. The Harry J. Stanley Assn. staged a "stupendous and magnificent musical revue and fashion promenade" in the park's mirrored ballroom during the week of April 16-21, 1928, featuring "the latest styles from Paris and New York displayed on beautiful models." Ballots for the most popular lady, policeman, fireman and association member were counted on closing night.

A life-long Elk who was president of the State Assn. in 1927, Guenther relished playing genial host to his fellow Elks. A. Harry Moore, Democratic guberna-

Beefsteak dinners were a Guenther tradition. From left to right, Henry Guenther, Commissioner August Lacombe and Commissioner Harry Stanley.

torial candidate, appeared at the Elks Mardi Gras in late October 1925. The 1926 Mardi Gras, a three-day event that drew some 10,000 people, featured a beauty contest and Halloween masquerade ball. Winner of the beauty contest received a diamond onyx ring and a silver loving cup. A Nash sedan and fully equipped hope chest were among the prizes awarded to winners of the masquerade ball.

The Elks annually joined forces with the N.J. Automobile Assn. to bring thousands of crippled children and orphans to the park for a free day-long outing. In 1922, the "kiddies" were brought to the park in 20 special trolley cars and 200 automobiles. Five hundred cars provided by Auto Club members transported some 3,000 children to the park in 1926. Orphan outings continued through the Twenties and Thirties, with most expenses underwritten by Guenther.

At mid-decade, Guenther announced the park's first Mardi Gras celebration, a week-long carnival designed to combat the traditional late August blahs. The park was gaily decorated with carnival bunting and strings of colored lights. Concessionaires wore outlandish costumes. Patrons dressed as their favorite characters from the movies or comic strips. "Olympic Park's Mardi Gras will take place from August 27 to September 3, and judging from the events, it will almost compare with that at Coney Island," reported the *Herald* in August 1928. "Two new numbers will be the bobbed hair contest and the perfect baby contest. The commercial parade Monday afternoon will

Herbert Baudistel

be the curtain raiser and after that it will be a case of gaiety, festivity and pleasure for the many thousands that take part. The parade each night, dancing, pie eating, watermelon, whistling, children's pet contests and swimming races are a few of the major events. The doll parade will be held on Wednesday afternoon and the baby parade, always a big feature, will take place on Friday afternoon. The bathing beauty contest will be decided on Labor day afternoon. The masque ball and crowning of the queen, who will be Miss Olive Anschuetz of Irvington, will take place Friday night." Twins Dorothy and Doris Thomas won first prize for costumes dressed as George and Martha Washington. Queen Olive received a gold watch, one of $5,000 in prizes awarded during Mardi Gras week.

The 1929 Mardi Gras featured a babies' health contest whose winner was proclaimed New Jersey's perfect baby. More than 100 mothers from Newark, Irvington and nearby suburbs entered their children in the contest. "Babies of every description there are, dimpled, roly-poly, some bubbling over with smiles, others cross and crying. One would have thought it was a contest for exercising lungs at the preliminary tests this week." Dr. Henry DeVincentis

of Newark examined the babies and was the judge, aided by a licensed nurse. "Joyce Hellwig. . .and Dolores Burrows were two of the smallest dimpled darlings. They are each four months old. Donald

Members of the Olympic Park Welfare Association, a group of park concessionaires, dressed up for Mardi Gras week, August 25-30, 1924. Harry A. Harris, second from right, second row, operated a "wheel stand" at the park for nearly 50 years.

Scenes from the 1930 Mardi Gras. ABOVE — Twenty prizes were awarded each evening for the prettiest and most original costumes. BELOW — An entry in the commercial float contest.

The Queen of the 1930 Mardi Gras seated on her throne, flanked by her court.

Henry Guenther crowns the Queen of the 1929 Mardi Gras.

Kyler. . .is a fat little rascal who weighs 22 pounds and 9 ounces. He is seven months old and thought it was great fun when the doctor put him in the baby scales." Doris Fried, 17 months old, "cried as though her heart would break when they put her on the table. Her little tears were soon wiped away when the doctor smiled at her."

To sustain interest, Guenther varied the Mardi Gras program each year. A pet contest judged by Guenther and McTague in 1929 drew a goat, two ducks and a mud turtle besides the expected assortment of snakes, lizards, cats, dogs, hamsters and parakeets. Other contests tried over the years with varying success included pie and watermelon eating and a miniature airplane race.

Olympic's Mardi Gras was the park's most popular feature for many years. "[T]he people, and particularly the young people, of Newark and its surrounding territory look forward to the Mardi Gras all year," wrote *Amusement Park Management* in 1931. "And, in the case of the young ladies, it is sometimes a case of planning and designing for many weeks. . . . There is perhaps no one thing that amusement parks can offer patrons that compares with a Mardi Gras. After all, patrons come to amusement parks to escape realities, to caper about and enjoy an atmosphere of fun and romance—in short, to live a different life and take on a different individuality for an all-too short a time." Mardi Gras week traditionally closed on Labor Day.

According to the magazine, the Mardi Gras Queen was chosen by Guenther himself, with a little help from his wife, "to do away with the various dissatisfactions and jealousies that crop out wherever beauties contest with one another." Explained the reporter: "Mr. Guenther frequents the ballroom now and then during the entire season. Among its girl patrons he finally selects two or three. . . . Finally, he calls Mrs. Guenther into consultation and between them they select the one to be honored. For several years a Mardi Gras king was also chosen but like many real ones in Europe, the king has been given the gate and now there is only the queen and her court. . . . The queen's throne is erected in the ballroom. She and her court form a procession through the park which ends at the ballroom," where the queen was crowned. A special 50 cent charge admitted patrons to the ballroom to view the week's festive climax.

Guenther employed a wide array of promotional ideas to lure customers through the gates. During each season there were two Three Cent Days, when everything in the park, including admission and refreshments, was three cents. Children under 10, usually admitted free, also ponied up their pennies to enter. As many as 30,000 patrons jammed the park's grounds on Three Cent Days.

On Dollar Days, tried experimentally in 1928 and 1929, each patron received 25 coupons good on anything anywhere in the park except the swimming pool and dance hall.

Henry C. Earle, a tenor who performed regularly at Newark's Mosque Theatre, led community singing every afternoon and evening during the late Twenties.

Fireworks at 11 o'clock on Friday evenings was another tradition. Miniature golf was introduced in 1927.

The Olympic Park ballroom, where Herbert Baudistel's Orchestra held sway, was a center of activity throughout the season. One of the best attended nights was Monday, Ladies Night, when all women were admitted free. On Thursday nights, through a tie-in with local merchants, silk hose and pumps were given away as prizes to the best dancers. Attendance quintupled on Silk Stocking Night. Baudistel's Orchestra was broadcast over the radio direct from Olympic Park three nights a week between 10:30 and 11 p.m. Weekly dancing lessons for children were free.

The ballroom's stage was also the site of the annual children's revue, with costumes and a good deal of prompting provided by the park and its staff. Beginning in 1930, proceeds of the revue were turned over to Irvington's unemployment relief fund.

The annual Swim Suit Review was one of park publicist Frank McTague's most popular innovations. McTague was a retired newspaperman. Marx's Department Store furnished the suits and paid the models.

Marx's Department Store at Irvington Centre sponsored the annual swim suit revue held from mid-June to mid-July. The store advertised for models and supplied the beach costumes and swimming suits. The ladies paraded under the watchful eye of Frank McTague, the park's veteran publicity man, on a platform erected in the picnic grove. Models were paid for their time and allowed to keep the suits they wore.

Guenther was very particular about the physical condition of the park. Grounds manager James F. Caffrey supervised a three-man clean-up crew that kept the grounds immaculate. Ride and attraction operators wore uniforms consisting of blue serge trousers and blouses, black ties and peaked caps. The rule that male patrons must wear a collar and tie was never relaxed an inch as long as Guenther was alive. Many were the young men who fashioned ties from shoe laces or bought their neckware at stands along the streets leading to the park's main gate.

The natural beauty of Becker's Grove, so much appreciated and nurtured by Herman Schmidt and Christian Kurz, was carefully maintained by Henry Guenther. "Mr. Guenther believes that the trees, as well as the flowers, are Olympic's most valuable assets," reported a trade journal in 1931. "Olympic Park raises its own trees, flowers and shrubbery. Located in its spacious grounds are its own hot houses and a tree nursery. . . ."

"One has only to walk through the park to see that this policy has been a great success. There can be few, if any, amusement parks that are more beautiful in shade trees, flowers and shrubbery, than is Olympic."

"Henry A. Guenther, himself, is a lover of flowers and devotes no little of his personal attention to their choice and development. The park itself is full of flower beds, rock gardens, flower boxes, hedges and shade trees. These greet you on the outside of the gate before you enter the park and after you have passed in the main entrance you see almost nothing but a cool and shady garden spot with no suggestion of commercial amusements."

"George Rathgerber, the gardener at Olympic, has an all year job. The first flowers grown in the Spring are tulips. From 5,000 to 10,000 bulbs are planted each year, many of them in beds near the main entrance. The colors used for the most part are yellow and new pink in combination and solid beds. Next comes the hyacinths in various colors. The flower beds themselves are in the form of crescents, anchors, butterflies, etc."

"One of the biggest hits that has been made yet by Olympic with flowers were the pansies that followed the hyacinths this year. Thousands of people came to the park to see them. Those who have been to Olympic in former seasons will note that Mr. Guenther is now devoting more of his park to flowers than ever before. Several concessions, buildings and booths were demolished this Spring and where they formerly stood are now flower beds."

"There is another interesting angle connected with the demolishing of the booths. They were broken up into firewood and unemployed and poor people were invited to come to the park and help themselves to the wood."

"It is very doubtful if there is a park in the United States that makes as much use of flowers as does Olympic. You will find flower boxes adorning the cashier boxes and you will find hedges and shrubbery hiding all mechanical parts of the rides or any other spot that might otherwise detract from the appearance of the park."

"Rock gardens are scattered through all parts of the park. In these are planted bleeding heart, begonias, geraniums, petunias, Sweet William and, as in the other flower beds, colored border plants. There are also ever live and poppies. There are 10,000 rose bushes in and around the park. Rambler roses climb the retaining wall that separates the two levels of the park. Hedges border almost all walks and are placed around rides and at any other advantageous point or locality. Almost all of these are grown from seedlings in the hothouse by Gardener Rathgerber."

"The visitor begins seeing Olympic's flowers before he enters the park. In front of the main entrance is the largest and most beautiful flower bed in the whole park. There is found the name 'Olympic Park' written in flowers and the plants are rotated according to the season."

"The shade trees are also grown from seedlings. The tree nursery is located in a spot back of the Custer Ride. Here can be seen trees in almost all stages of growth from seedlings to half grown trees. For the most part they are maples, spruce, and poplars. Much care is devoted to the shade trees of the park and the result is that it is difficult to find a healthier or more beautiful group of trees anywhere."

Regular concerts were performed by the park's own band three times a day in the white bandstand in the grove. Joe Basile, hired to lead the park's brass band in 1922, played to hundreds of thousands of fans until his death in 1961. Special musical attractions during the Twenties included the Royal Scotch Highlanders Band, an internationally-famous 30-piece bagpipe unit that arrived in Newark in a "specially decorated Pullman car trimmed and painted in a most picturesque manner." Creatore and his

Olympic Park BEAUTIFUL

THE MOST BEAUTIFUL
AMUSEMENT PARK
IN NEW JERSEY

Thrilling
ROLLER COASTER
A WILD RIDE
OVER THE TREETOPS ETC.

WHIP
THE SNAPPY RIDE

ACCOMPLISHED MUSICIANS
IN ATTENDANCE

DANCE PAVILION DE LUXE

THE LARGEST
IN THE EAST

PALACE of FUN
25 AMUSEMENTS
UNDER ONE ROOF

Olympic Park

BEAUTIFUL

THE MOST BEAUTIFUL
AMUSEMENT PARK
IN NEW JERSEY

FINEST **RESTAURANT** FACILITIES

FERRIS WHEEL   AERIAL SENSATION   AEROPLANE SWING

CHILDREN'S PLAYGROUND AND MOTHER'S REST   REFRESHMENTS AND LUNCH ROOM   FREE SWINGS—SLIDES—SANDPITS ETC.

FROLIC
SOMETHING DIFFERENT

DODGEM
THE GREATEST SENSATION OF THE YEAR

BILLIARDS ETC.

BOWLING

An aerial view taken in 1929. The new baseball stadium is at lower left, next to it is the Diplodocus, and at lower right, the roller coaster. Bordering the park to the west was a creek, clearly outlined in this photo by a row of trees.

band visited Olympic Park direct from Atlantic City's Million Dollar Pier in July 1928 for a week's engagement. His 44 musicians played four concerts daily. "The soprano soloist is Pauline Talma, who has the reputation of being the best dressed woman on the concert stage," reported the *Herald.* "It is said she never wears the same gown twice during a week's engagement." The Svengali of the Baton, as Creatore was known, featured the music of Verdi, Wagner and Sousa.

One of the most fanciful of the park's attractions made its debut in May 1928 when a new fun house, Blue Beard's Palace, flung open its doors. "During the past several week-ends it has been stormed with patrons and pronounced one of the most up-to-date amusement devices in this vicinity," raved the local press. "With its high towers and mysterious rooms set among rocky cliffs beautified in an artistic manner with pretty sunken gardens and fountain, it makes a picturesque scene."

According to the paper, the scenes included "the estate of Bluebeard showing the racing stables complete in minute detail, wine cellar showing casks of liquor, jugs of rum [and] bottles of gin over which the enforcement authorities have no control. Bluebeard is shown very much intoxicated and dreaming of his pretty wives."

The park was thoroughly overhauled for the 1929 season. Olympic's two roller coasters, the Diplodocus and Jack Rabbit, and the Custer cars were renovated by lengthening the track and adding more cars. A pig slide and upside-down house were added to the fun plaza and the latest model Scrambler installed. A new $50,000 baseball stadium and merry-go-round greeted visitors when the gates opened on May 25. To provide "adequate accommodations for the rapidly growing auto trade," reported *Billboard,* "an artistic gate has been erected at the 40th Street entrance for both autos and pedestrians."

9

THE LARGEST POOL
IN THE EAST

The park's most popular postwar attraction was its pool, an Olympic-size concrete extravaganza billed as "The Largest Swimming Pool in the East." Big enough to accommodate 5,000 bathers at a time, the pool's sparkling blue water and white sand beach drew 160,000 to 170,000 people annually in the Thirties and Forties, and nearly as many in later years. A dependable drawing card each of the 43 seasons it was in operation, the Olympic Park pool repaid its $300,000 initial cost many times over, although curiously enough, many of the investors who helped build it never saw a dime.

Herman Schmidt dreamed of a pool as early as 1914 but lacked the capital to build one. The Guenthers advertised a swimming pool site "as a concession in the best park in the East" in *Billboard* magazine in the fall of 1919, but there were no takers. Three years later, with the Roaring Twenties gathering steam, a group of enthusiastic New York investors formed the Olympic Natatorium Corporation. Signing a 20-year lease with Guenther, they sold $220,000 worth of stock, much of it to small investors in Newark and Irvington. Headed by New Yorkers Sidney Reynolds, president of World Wide Amusement Co., John O'Brien, associated with Amusement Builders Corp., and John R. Walker, a businessman, the corporation promoted the pool's investment potential as well as the healthful aspects of swimming. J. Herbert Reed, president of the Newark Athletic Club, and several area businessmen

joined the enterprise. "At last!" cried the ads, "An outdoor swimming pool only a half hour from the Four Corners! You are invited to join prominent businessmen of Newark in financing this pool. An investment in the Olympic Park Natatorium Corporation's shares should yield big profits for years to come. . . . An investment in the Olympic Natatorium Corporation not only entitles you to a share of the profits of the entire enterprise, but gives you a membership in the Olympic Natatorium Association and the privilege of enjoying the pool without additional expense for 20 years." The stock sold quickly as investors dreamed of healthy bodies and bulging bank accounts.

Work on the pool began Feb. 19, 1923, when the first of 26,000 cubic yards of earth and rock were excavated. Construction, which took four and a half months to complete, required 4,800 barrels of cement, 11 miles of pipe for water, gas, electric and sanitary lines and 7,000 lights for night bathing. A sand beach at the shallow end of the pool consumed 18,050 tons of white sand shipped from Rockaway Beach, Long Island. By March, when the old race track had become a shapeless mud hole, the local press carried its first detailed account of the pool project:

"The pool will be 400 feet long and 200 feet wide and will vary in depth from a few inches to nine and a half feet. It will accommodate about 4,000 bathers at one time and will be one of the largest swimming

Who is the best swimmer in your family?

EVERY member of the family should be able to swim—not only for the pleasure and exercise swimming and diving affords, but because occasions arise when a good swimmer can save the lives of others and at the same time insure his or her own safety. There will be FREE SWIMMING INSTRUCTION at the new Olympic Pool, enabling Association members to become good swimmers. Every provision is being made for the comfort and safety of all who take advantage of the big, clean pool.

400x200-FOOT POOL
5,000 BATHERS
CAN ENJOY A SWIM WITHOUT OVERCROWDING

OLYMPIC SWIMMING POOL

THERE ARE
1,000 Bath Houses
and 1,000 Lockers also many private rooms that may be rented for the season.

At last! An outdoor swimming pool only a half hour from the Four Corners! The Olympic Natatorium Corporation, under the direction of some of Newark's leading business men is rapidly bringing to completion this wonderful pool in Olympic Park, Irvington.

Among the amusements will be good music, radio concerts, a giant sea swing, a wading pool for the kiddies and a big white, sandy beach.

Arrangements have been made to bring swimmers of international prominence to the Olympic Pool, and the plans include swimming races, polo games, water carnivals and diving contests. There will be seats for 5,000 spectators.

There will also be a fine restaurant, a barber shop, valet service and a beauty parlor with electric hair dryers for the ladies.

Extraordinary Investment Opportunity!
Worth While Dividends Assured Investors in This Popular Venture

You are invited to join prominent business men of Newark in financing this Pool. An investment in the Olympic Natatorium Corporation's shares should yield big profits for years to come. Our Prospectus outlines construction and operating costs in detail. This will be sent to you upon request. The Pool is now being constructed and should be in a position to earn handsome dividends. It fills a long-felt need in Greater Newark and is sure to enjoy tremendous patronage.

Quick Action Necessary

An investment in the Olympic Natatorium Corporation not only entitles you to a share of the profits of the entire enterprise, but gives you a membership in the Olympic Natatorium Association and the privilege of enjoying the pool without additional expense for 20 years. Our list of directors and stockholders includes many of our leading business men and indications points to all shares being subscribed in the very near future, so we advise you to investigate at once.

Mail Coupon Below for Full Particulars

DIRECTORS

FARLEY OSGOOD
Vice-Pres. and General Manager Public Service Electric Co.

J. HERBERT REID
President, Newark Athletic Club

CORBETT McCARTHY
Vice-Pres. and General Manager Hahne & Co.

JOHN MacARTHUR
President Williams Baking Co.

JOHN O'BRIEN
Treasurer Amusement Builders' Corporation, New York

SIDNEY REYNOLDS
President World Wide Amusement Co., New York

MAIL THIS COUPON NOW!
Olympic Natatorium Corporation
Forty Park Place, Newark, N. J.

Please furnish me, without obligation on my part, complete information about the Olympic Swimming Pool and how to become a member of the Olympic Natatorium Association, which will entitle me to free use of swimming pool and bathhouses for twenty years.

Name ....

Address ....

pools in the East. It will contain 3,750,000 gallons of water. The water will be taken from the pool and go through five filters by electrically driven pumps once every 20 hours. After passing through the filters, it will be treated by the violet ray. As a further precaution against bacteria, the water will before being returned to the pool, be further treated by chlorinators, the system of purifying creating a water which will be purer for bathing purposes than the actual water used for drinking purposes."

"There will be 1,000 individual bath houses and 3,000 lockers, and in addition there will be 170 individual rooms. Above the bath houses and lockers will be a series of bleachers forming an amphitheatre around three sides of the pool. These seats will accommodate 5,000 spectators for the swimming races, water polo, and other water sports which will be held in the pool. The pool will provide facilities for a 100-yard dash race, and will be the only pool in the East having this capacity. All races will be held under the auspices of the [Newark] Amateur Athletic Union."

"At the shallow end of the pool a sea swing will be installed and will furnish the last word in thrills to the bather. A restaurant will cater to the requirements of the bathers and spectators and there will also be a beauty parlor for the ladies, equipped with electric hair dryers. For the men patrons there will be a barber shop, shoe shining parlor and valet service. The smallest children will not be overlooked, as a wading pool with a few inches of water will be available for them. A sand beach 165 feet long and 135 feet wide will bring the seashore to Olympic Park."

"Arrangements have been made to bring to the Olympic Pool nationally known swimmers both men and women, amateurs and professionals, so that the patrons of the pool will be able to see the holders of

records which have been made in other pools and which the management hope will be made over in Olympic Park. The entire pool will be under the management of H.C. Wilson, who was an important factor in making the huge success achieved at Madison Square Garden. He will have a competent corps of assistants, life guards, and the comfort and enjoyment of the patrons of the pool will be the only object desired by the Olympic Natatorium Corporation."

Water began flowing into the pool at the end of June, a process that took nearly 10 days to complete. Fearing the loss of pressure in its entire system, the water company insisted that the pool be filled only during late evening hours.

The public took its first dip in the pool on July 4, 1923, following a water carnival that starred world-champion swimmer Johnny Weismuller, his brother, Peter, and Gertrude Ederle and Aileen Riggin of the New York Women's Swimming Assn. Weismuller, who later won fame as Hollywood's Tarzan, came within seconds of equalling his previous world's rec-

A capacity audience crowded the pool for opening day ceremonies, July 4, 1923. Johnny Weismuller and Gertrude Ederle were among the star athletes on hand for the festivities.

Pool lifeguards in 1936 were (left to right) *Jack Daly, Bill Waldron, Don Chalmers, Maurie Sapienza, Ray Wilner and John Winter.*

ord in the 50-yard and 300-meter races. To the disappointment of the inaugural crowd, diving competitions scheduled for the day had to be called off because the pool was less than three-quarters filled.

A bitter trolley strike that began on Aug. 1 and lasted well into September cut attendance at the park to record-low numbers. Pool admissions, which had swelled during July, plummeted in August and September. Less than two months after the pool opened, the corporation was unable to meet its payroll. With more than 100 creditors screaming for payment, the court was forced to intervene, appointing Henry Guenther receiver of the corporation in October. A year later when the receivership ended, Guenther was named president of the Natatorium Corporation and his brother, Anthony, manager of the pool. Despite their best efforts, however, the pool failed to turn a profit. During the next two decades, lawyers, judges, creditors and stock and bondholders picked over the Natatorium Corporation's affairs, trying to staunch the flow of red ink, generally without success. The enormous cost of construction, maintenance and interest payments was more than the enterprise could support, even when pool attendance was high. From 1924 to 1931, when investors again sought court intervention, the corporation lost more than $156,000.

Pool manager Joseph H. Palmer.

The women's gate, Summer 1930.

Looking north, c. 1935.

A water polo game in progress, August 1942.

The pool was 9 ft. deep near the water wheel.

South end of the pool.

The diving raft, c. 1950.

Pool pals, c. 1941.

On the beach at Olympic Park, c. 1930.

The thousands of swimmers and sunbathers who enjoyed the pool daily were blissfully ignorant of the endless financial and legal tangles that beset the Natatorium Corporation. To them nothing was more important than a clear sky, bright sun and a cool breeze. Henry and Anthony Guenther ran the pool with the same commitment to wholesome family entertainment that characterized the rest of Olympic Park. After Anthony Guenther died in March 1934, succeeding pool managers, including Joseph H. Palmer, John Bedell and Harold Scott, maintained the same high standards. The pool itself was kept immaculate. It was drained and cleaned annually and every five years or so another thousand tons of white sand was trucked in to renew the large beach. In 1931, after a 300-foot deep well was sunk, city water was no longer used. For many years, men and women entered through gates on opposite sides of the pool, a practice abandoned after World War II. Life guards had strict instructions to enforce the rules against two-piece bathing suits, hugging and kissing and rowdy conduct. Offenders were swiftly evicted. Admission was 50 cents on weekdays and $1 on weekends and holidays. Children paid a quarter.

After the Depression struck, admission fees were cut nearly in half. In 1932, Sunday swimming was reduced to 55 cents. Towels and swimsuits were rented for a dime. Local youngsters enrolled through the Irvington or Maplewood recreation departments used the pool without charge on weekday mornings. Newark youngsters could swim for a dime on Monday, Wednesday and Friday mornings. Those from Irvington and Maplewood used the pool on Tuesday, Thursday and Saturday. Members of the pool's Teen Club, active in the Fifties and Sixties, swam at reduced rates.

During the pool's 43 seasons, an estimated five million admissions were recorded. Only seven persons drowned, a safety record attributable to a well-trained crew of life-guards who maintained a close watch over the pool's eight diving boards, central diving platform and 80,000 square feet of surface area. The pool was open seven days a week from 9a.m. to 9p.m. and as late as 11p.m. on extremely hot nights.

Moonlight bathing was extremely popular during the Thirties, when a day at the Olympic Park pool was the only vacation many families could afford.

Two of the pool's 8 diving platforms, c. 1950, from a postcard.

"A night in Hawaii," held in mid-July 1933, was a typical Guenther promotion: "Visitors are invited to wear their most picturesque pajamas and swimming togs and it is suggested [that] Neptune's 'chillun' bring their ukeleles, banjos, guitars and mandolins to help along the merriment under the light of two moons—Luna herself and a synthetic silvery moon provided by the management."

Johnny Weismuller returned to the pool several times before Hollywood lured him out of the water and into the trees. In July 1930, the "dean of swimmers" put on an exhibition before several thousand. "Pop Neptune's right hand man, considered second to none in the water, exhibited a variety of strokes and clowned in a way on the diving boards that would make many a clown envious," reported the *Herald*. "He won the hearts of the onlookers by his easy machine-like movements in the water. Weismuller is very easy to look at from the standpoint of physique. He credits his wonderful build to swimming."

The Zittenfeld Twins, Doris and Phyllis, "the 14-year-old wonder swimmers," appeared in exhibition at the pool in August 1928. The "Zitz," rated among America's best female swimmers, gained their reputation by swimming from New York's Battery to Boston.

Learning to swim was easy at the Olympic Park pool. During the Thirties and Forties, the Newark *Sunday Call* sponsored free learn to swim classes for

The Learn to Swim program, sponsored by the Irvington Chapter of the American Red Cross, produced these trophy winners in the mid-Fifties. At left is Harold Scott, pool director, and at right rear is Angela DiCostanzo, chief instructor. Between Scott and DiCostanzo are Lynn Ketchow and Miriam Budney.

90

4th to 9th graders. In the Forties, Fifties and Sixties, the Red Cross sponsored a two-month water safety and learn to swim course that annually enrolled 1,500 to 2,000 boys and girls of school age. Certificates and trophies were awarded to senior life savers, water safety aides, junior life savers and advanced swimmers. Scuba diving classes were added in 1962 under the auspices of the Irvington Fire Department.

Water sports played a large role in boosting pool attendance for many years. Four meets were held in the summer of 1934 under the sponsorship of the Newark Women's Athletic Club, beginning with a gala water carnival and ending with a meet that included "all the leading mermaids of the East." Featured events were the 100-meter freestyle senior men's championship and the 50-meter junior championship for women. National water polo matches under AAU auspices were staged during World War II. During the Forties, the *Sunday Call*, in conjunction with the Newark Athletic Club, published reduced admission coupons to both the park and pool. On Sunday Call Day, the girls swimming team of the Newark A.C. performed "aquatic ballets and classic water group maneuvers." Sunday Call Day on July 30, 1945, was typical: "Steve Ellis, dance

band announcer at WPAT, will be master of ceremonies for the full program, which will include personal appearances of stage, radio and screen personalities," said the paper. "Stan Kenton and his orchestra, currently playing at the Meadowbrook, will be on hand for the occasion." The New Jersey Association of the AAU sponsored junior and senior diving and outdoor synchronized swimming meets at the park until it closed. In 1960, the U.S. Olympic swimming team appeared at the pool before heading to Rome for the quadrennial games.

Bathing beauty contests for girls from two to 20 at pool side were a fixture every season. Winners of the seven weekly contests held in July and August competed against each other on the last Thursday before Labor Day for the title of Miss Olympic Park Pool. Trophies were awarded to girls in three age groups, from two through eight, nine through 13 and those over 13.

The pool was a source of enormous pleasure to the tens of thousands who swam its sparkling waters each season. For the children, it was a place to build sand-castles on the beach or wade in the shallow end under the watchful eye of mom or dad. Teenagers learned to swim there or gathered with their school-

Sometimes the beach was so crowded there was barely room to spread a blanket. From a postcard, c. 1950.

mates during the long summer vacation. Sunbathing, swimming or plain relaxing were the pool's main attractions for adults. Many youngsters from Newark, Irvington, Maplewood and surrounding communities virtually grew up at the Olympic Park pool. June Simon Mericle, whose parents operated the Pony Track at the park for nearly a decade, lived across the street from the main gate: "My earliest memories of the pool go back to the late Thirties, when I was no more than 10 or 11 years old. Money was scarce in those days and we had to earn the quarter it cost to get in the pool. My friends and I were an enterprising lot. Five or six of us from the neighborhood set up three stands on 43rd Street, using orange crates and some old boards. Two of the stands were games of chance. I ran the "Guess Your Age" stand and I remember how impressed my mother was with my talent. Prizes were no problem. We simply entered the park early in the morning before the cleanup crews made their rounds, rummaging through the trash cans for discarded souvenirs or slum plaster from the night before. As soon as we each earned 25 cents, we collapsed our stands, hid them away and went swimming in the pool."

The beach, with the Midway in the background, 1961.

10

LOWER PRICES AND TIGHTENED BELTS

The Roaring Twenties died a sudden death in late October 1929 when the New York Stock Market crash wiped out more than $30 billion in the space of a few days. Slowly at first and then with gathering speed, the spectre of depression spread across the nation. Newark and its suburbs were hit full-force in the fall of 1930 when some 50,000 people were on relief. By 1933, area payrolls stood at 45 percent of their 1925 levels and per capita income was roughly half of what it had been in 1929. In Newark, men sold apples in the streets, or begged. In Irvington, where the unemployed earned $4 a day cutting old telephone poles into kindling, every town employee paid more than $1,040 annually took a 10 percent salary cut.

Olympic Park experienced the first effects of the depression in 1931 when receipts dropped some 10 percent. By 1933, income was down 25 percent from 1930, the park's best year, and rumors that Henry Guenther was on the verge of bankruptcy were commonplace. Olympic weathered the storm partly because the park was inexpensive and convenient for day-trippers, partly because its owner was an indominable optimist who could write, as Guenther did in June 1933 to the owner of a park in the mid-west: "From present indications, I believe things might be better in July and August because various manufacturers are putting on additional help and, strange to say, are maintaining former wage scales." In truth, Olympic Park's receipts never reached the levels attained in the Twenties until the outbreak of World War II. Lower prices, tightened belts and a blizzard of new but generally inexpensive attractions kept the crowds coming, although at reduced levels, during the park's most trying decade.

The 1930 season opened on May 25 with National Turner's Day, an afternoon and evening of pyramid building, drills, tumbling and exercises on the horse, buck, horizontal and parallel bars by girls and boys six years and up. Regular features that year included the swimming pool, a new 18-hole miniature golf course, band concerts afternoons and evenings augmented by recorded music "on the Victor orthophonic," free circus and dancing classes in the ballroom. Circus week, scheduled for the July 4th holiday, featured "Babe," an elephant that danced the Charleston and the shimmy, and Roberta's Animals, complete with a bucking mule, ponies, dogs and monkeys in "an exhibition of side-splitting propensities." The park's first Three-Cent Day of the season came in mid-July, followed a week later by Shriner's Day under the auspices of Newark's Salaam Temple, assisted by the Crescent Temple of Trenton. More than 10,000 Masons and their friends attended. Polish Day, a charity event sponsored by 70 Essex County Polish-American organizations, followed a week later.

The "most elaborate bathing suit revue ever staged in this vicinity" opened on June 14, featuring "twelve attractive and shapely girls" modelling B.V.D. bathing attire from Hahne's Department Store. In the ballroom, dancing instructor Thomas Edward Parson guided would-be terpsichoreans through their paces. Free instructions in "modernistic dancing" were offered on Tuesday evenings, free dancing classes for children on Saturday afternoons. Monday was Ladies' Night, Wednesday, Collegiate Contest Night. Miss Nell Rose was crowned carnival queen of the annual Mardi Gras, held from Sept. 1 to 7.

Tuscan Dairy Farms, a 700-cow dairy located in nearby Union, hosted several thousand people on Aug. 27 when a Tuscan milk bottle cap was good for free admission to the park and on most rides. "Get a free ride at the Olympic Park amusement attractions Tuesday by drinking more milk," proclaimed the *Herald*. "Believe it or not, kiddies as well as grown-ups can make whoopee without cost providing they imbibe generously of the lacteal fluid." One hundred and fifty baskets filled with Tuscan milk, cream, butter, pot cheese, buttermilk and sour cream were raffled off.

Admission was free again on Sept. 2 when Guenther staged his first (and last, at it turned out) Reciprocity Day. Holders of special newspaper coupons could ride five rides without charge in what the park's management called "this method of showing its appreciation of the splendid support and cooperation of its many patrons.'"

Crown jewel of the 1930 season was the appearance of John Philip Sousa and his band on Sunday, Aug. 25. It was Sousa's fourth and final concert at the park and for the thousands who attended the performances at 3, 5, 8, and 11p.m., it was a memorable occasion. "There will be no extra charge with free seats 'neath the tall shade trees," announced the local newspaper. "Manager Guenther is anxious that the kiddies and the folks whose income will not permit them to pay fancy prices, be enabled to see and hear the noted composer and warrior without extra cost. It is one of the few occasions where Sousa permits it." The program included Sousa's newest marches, "The Royal Welsh Fusiliers," "Washington Bi-Centennial," "Daughters of Texas," "Salvation Army" and the "Harmonica Wizard." Sousa, who was then 76 and already a legend in his own lifetime, was to die less than two years later.

Leaping Lena, a rearing, leaping auto ride, was invented by James A. Sherry and installed in 1926. The Olympic Park installation was the first in the nation.

ABOVE — *Felix Fox, his daughter, Margaret, and sons, Felix Jr. and Patrick, are at the wheels of their Custer Cars in this early Thirties photo. The miniature cars were equipped with 3 hp. gasoline motors and could do 5 mph. Fox, who was later to open 8 paint stores in Essex and Monmouth Counties, virtually launched his career as a painting contractor at Olympic Park in 1926. At the same time he operated several stands and boosted business at the Haunted Castle by amplifying the screams of patrons inside.* BELOW — *Blue Beard's Palace made its debut in 1928 with moving stairs, walls and ceilings, a crooked room, a huge exit slide (you could rent coveralls) and a floor board that flew up and whacked your posterior when you stepped on it. The board was removed after one too many law suits.*

Captain Joe Basile

"One thrill after the other appears to be the policy adopted by Manager Guenther of Olympic Park," reported the press in June 1931 when The Great Alfred, dubbed "The Demon of the Air," opened for a week's run at the free circus. Following Alfred's "amazing array of hazardous feats" on the swinging trapeze and rings came Carlos' Comedy Circus; Captain Charles' leaping hounds; the Sensational Valentines, known in the circus world as the "wizards of the whirling spectacle;" the Great Candall, a comic bare-backed rider; and, in August, the Looping Nixes, a show billed as "the King of the Thrills and the last word in motor madness." According to the papers, the Nixes "will ride high powered racing motorcycles 16 feet in the air upside down in a beautiful plated lattice cage."

Other attractions in 1931 were Joe Basile and his Madison Square Garden Band, with Miss Edna Joyce, soloist, a tomato eating championship sponsored by the Boy Scouts, and a fireworks spectacular mounted by Thearle-Duffield entitled "The Last Days of Pompeii," presented in mid-August. The Thearle-Duffield extravaganza drew nearly 40,000 to the park, almost as many as the Sousa concert the year before. The park's free fireworks had been popular for years but on July 4, 1931, a record crowd of 50,000 viewed the pyrotechnics. So large was the attendance that the automobile gates had to be closed for the first time in the park's history. Recognizing a good thing when he saw it, Guenther exhibited fireworks every Tuesday and Thursday night throughout the remainder of the season.

The week of July 6 was Astor House Coffee Week, with free baskets of groceries given away daily. Depression-era crowds, happy to take home tens of thousands of cute but useless trinkets each season, appreciated the more practical prizes that began to appear on the park's many stands. Coffee, sugar and crackers were soon every bit as popular as the standard plaster Betty Boop and Mae West statuette or the ubiquitous Kewpie doll.

In late August, the National Association of Amusement Parks convened its summer meeting at Olympic Park.

The 1931 season closed on a fragrant note with the Northern Jersey Flower Show, held on Sept. 16 and 17 under the auspices of the N.J. Dahlia Society, Federated Garden Clubs and N.J. Assn. of Nurserymen. Nearly 10,000 visitors admired 2,300 floral exhibits, including "bowers of vari-colored dahlias."

To promote business during the Depression, Guenther booked Olympic's largest rodeo show ever for 10 days in July 1932. California Frank's Rodeo arrived by train on the 15th: "In the wee

June and Lois Simon in a racing car used by the Daring Dobishes in 1933.

An open air trolley of the No. 25 Springfield Avenue line enters Irvington on its way to Olympic Park, June 20, 1934.

Carol Woodhead, age 2, winner in the Most Beautiful Brunette category, 1933 Baby Parade.

hours of the morning, residents of Irvington were startled from a sound sleep by the squealing of out-law horses and the long-drawn bellow of wild steers as they were herded through the streets toward Olympic Park," reported the newspaper. "At day-break cowboys and cowgirls were unloading 150 head of wild stock from the baggage cars on the Le-high Valley Railroad, into the corrals, where they were bunched and headed toward the park. Half way to the park, two Brahma steers took to battling and for a time it looked like the whole herd would stampede. The two Brahma stags have been brew-ing trouble since they were shipped from the big ranch of California Frank." Elmo Carr, chief of the cowboys (every inch as good a publicity agent as Frank McTague), explained that "some day these two will finally settle their troubles when one or the other will be gored to death. When two Brahma steers get to making war on each other there is bound to be serious trouble among the herd."

Wild steer riding was just one of the many thrilling events of the show. The two battling "mighty mon-archs of the herd" were among a dozen bulls that came charging out of the chutes with a rider on their backs twice daily to the amusement of large crowds. Sadly, the Brahmas refused to "settle their troubles" before the expectant onlookers.

At the end of July, Guenther dropped the admis-sion price of the pool to 55 cents in an effort to en-courage attendance. In August, he added a treasure hunt to the pool's attractions. Each day, 10 tokens redeemable in cash were scattered about the pool.

The Northern New Jersey Agricultural Fair and Exposition, held Sept. 19-25, brought the year to a bucolic close. Exhibits of vegetables, fruits, flowers, cattle, horses, poultry, swine, pigeons, rabbits, bees and dogs filled the grove, while a display of agricultural machinery and automobiles occupied the ballroom.

A three-day flower show hosted by the Northern New Jersey Garden Club heralded the park's 1933 season, followed two weeks later by a free kiddie outing sponsored by the August L. Lacombe Assn. "Fat kiddies, thin kiddies, curly heads, red heads

site of the Miss New Jersey 1933 contest. "Scores of gorgeous girls, delightful eyefuls" competed for the right to represent the state in the Miss America Contest held in Atlantic City.

Jack Snow, billed as the "Man Who Is Buried Alive," drew gawkers by the hundreds. Housed in a room six feet below the surface, Snow set out to beat the national record for live burial, although whether he succeeded has been lost in the mists of history. Communicating with the surface by telephone and fed via a dumbwaiter, Snow listened to the radio, exercised with dumbbells and read the newspaper in his subterranean chamber for at least a month. For a

Baby Parade contestants, 1930 Mardi Gras.

and freckle-faced youngsters" were among 5,000 boys and girls noisily vying for 600 prizes, free balloons and candy. Prudently, the association arranged to have three nurses and a doctor on hand for emergencies.

Guenther's fertile imagination ranged far and wide for gimmicks that might bolster sagging attendance. Bingo arrived at Olympic in the shape of a large (and very hot) canvas tent. Crowded with bleacher seats for the players, many of whom returned day after day, week after week, to compete for prize baskets filled with groceries, the tent quickly gave way to the more spacious ballroom, where games were held until they were banned by the County Prosecutor in 1939. On Aug. 28 the park was the

nickel, patrons could watch Snow's antics through a periscope.

A few hundred feet from Snow's burial site was the park's fabulous electric fountain, installed in 1933. Equipped with hundreds of colored lights, the fountain put on a dazzling show every hour on the hour after dusk. Said the Newark *News*: "Five hundred gallons per minute pour into the fountain—and as it leaps under the brilliant lights into the air while living models pose as famous pieces of statuary or figures in noted paintings, it presents novel and picturesque effects." A concealed platform elevator lifted the model, demurely attired in a one-piece bathing suit, six feet into the air as the fountain erupted, creating the illusion that she had risen from

ABOVE — *Conductor Joe Basile in the grove with his Olympic Park Band, 1931.* BELOW — *Finalists in the 1930 Mardi Gras Beauty Contest primp for the camera.*

THE WORLDS PENDULUM

the spray.

The Junior Order's annual outing on Sept. 5-9 brought the season to a close as usual, although with a different twist in 1933. Echoing President Franklin Roosevelt's call for a "Buy, Build and Boost Campaign," the Junior Order built a one-family bungalow on Hoover Place in Irvington, hiring unemployed tradesmen. "The Prosperity Home," as it was called, was raffled off on the outing's closing day.

The nation was still in the grips of the Depression when the 1934 season, the worst in the park's history, opened on Memorial Day. Nothing daunted, Guenther searched for new promotions, including distribution of an ever-increasing array of cheap souvenirs. During the Thirties, park patrons were deluged with mirrors, lead pencils, wooden whistles, celluloid pipes, erasers, paper guns, bridge and golf pencils, tin frogs, blotters and celluloid toothpick holders, all proclaiming Olympic the "Greatest Amusement Park in New Jersey." New diving boards were installed in the pool to accommodate the popular championship swim meets and the dance hall was refurbished.

In July, the park scheduled the first of a series of

LEFT — *An elaborate entry in 1930's Mardi Gras Baby Parade.* BELOW — *Two-year-old Nancy Faupel garners first prize as Snow White in the 1939 Baby Parade.*

weekly spelling bees run by Guenther's sons, Robert and Henry Jr. Charles B. Kelly, a Union High School teacher, won first prize of $10.

August was contest month, with a mutt show on Aug. 11, a hobby show on the 15th, a "mutt show for cats" on the 18th and the annual baby parade on Aug. 25. The baby parade, with cash awards for the finest float and the most beautiful, healthiest and peppiest babies, drew several hundred contestants. Chief judge was WOR's Uncle Don, "the kiddie's pal," whose 6p.m. radio show was a ritual to some five million area youngsters.

Uncle Don, who returned to the park each year through the early Forties, sang, thumped the piano and told cute stories about two unruly tikes named Willapuss-Wallapuss and Suzan-Beduzin, just the way he did every evening on network radio.

Following the baby parade, dance teacher Lillian Daniels presented her final production of the summer season, a minstrel show with a cast recruited from park patrons and their children. "One hundred and twenty-five kiddies are engaged in this extravaganza," said the *Herald.* "New songs, original costumes and breezy dancing will feature this pretentious production."

Nineteen days of pony express races scheduled to begin in mid-July 1935, were banned by the court after the State Racing Commission refused to grant a license. Guenther and Douglas Hertz, the promoter, argued in vain that the pony races were a "contest of endurance for the jockeys," who had to change mounts every two and half minutes. No betting would be permitted, Guenther assured the authorities, but neither the Racing Commission nor the court were persuaded and the ban remained.

During the Fourth of July fireworks display, an aerial bomb skipped along the ground into the crowd instead of sailing into the air. Five spectators were burned, none seriously, when the rocket exploded.

Grand opera returned to Olympic Park on Sept. 15 when American Legion Post 16 sponsored a performance of "Cavalleria Rusticana" and "Pagliacci" by the Puccini Grand Opera Co. Fulgenzio Guerrieri, the well-known maestro, directed a cast of 50.

Nazi Germany cast its shadow over Olympic Park in May 1936 when the German-American League of Essex County announced plans for an athletic contest and concert to benefit the American Olympic Fund, then raising money to send a team to the Berlin Olympic Games. Co-sponsored by the New Jersey branch of the AAU, the festival was set for May 17. "We are convinced that through sending of American athletic teams to the Olympic Games," wrote the sponsors, "an understanding for the economical and political problems of the New Germany will be aroused."

The American League Against War and Fascism, opposed to American participation in the Olympic Games, demanded that Guenther cancel the festival. "If you permit the German-American League to hold this celebration you will be violating the tradition of a fun spot," wrote Mrs. Frances Dodge, se-

Lillian Daniels' School of the Dance after a performance of "The Good Ship Olympic," its 1936 production. See page 169 for more about the show.

ABOVE — *The Springfield Avenue trolley departs the 43rd Street gate.* BELOW — *Jeanne Toombs, age 3, costumed as the Campbell's Soup Kid for the 1934 Baby Parade. Note the 3¢ Day sign at the rear.*

cretary to the League. "There can't be fun where the shadow of the Nazi hangman hovers over the American athlete." The German-American League for Culture and the Friends of Democracy joined the protest.

As May 17 approached, rumors flew that anti-Nazis would disrupt the festival. Described in an FBI report as a "hot-bed" of German-American Bund activity, Irvington counted perhaps as many as 500 Bund members. Held despite the protests, the festival attracted about 3,000 visitors. Weight lifting, handball, soccer and volleyball contests occupied the afternoon, a military band concert and music by the United Singers, Newark Saengerchor and the Vereinigte Damenchor the evening. Ten special officers stood guard, ready to evacuate the park at the first hint of trouble.

The dance hall auditorium was crowded with concert-goers when restaurant manager Nicholas Giuliano heard the crackling of flames a few minutes after 10p.m. Seconds later the lights went out and the auditorium filled with smoke, scattering the panicky crowd. Damage was moderate and there were only a few minor injuries, as the fire was soon quelled. Investigators attributed the flames to paint and turpentine stored in the restaurant, which was being redecorated. Festival sponsors claimed that the enemies of the New Germany were the culprits.

The remainder of the 1936 season proceeded on a calmer note. In July, the Federal Theatre delighted youngsters with a month-long series of free marion-

ABOVE — *Electric sign at the Four Corners, Newark, seen by 300,000 people a day.* BELOW — *The park's miniature train waits for passengers near the Jack Rabbit, 1930.*

A toast at the first annual outing of the Waiters' and Cooks' Union Local 109 and Bartenders' Union Local 131, August 27, 1934. E. L. Loucopoulos, chairman of the event, stands third from right, rear.

ette plays, including "Molly Pitcher" and "The Enchanted House," an Oriental fairy tale.

Prizefighter Jack Dempsey was one of the judges of the 1936 baby parade.

Area Republicans scheduled a "monster rally" in support of the Landon-Knox ticket on Oct. 1 after the regular season ended. Later that month, Putt Mossman, "motorcycle stunt specialist," headed a group of visiting racers in a combination trick and race meet at the Olympic Park stadium. "The former world's champion horse-pitcher and self-styled champion stunt motorcyclist will make a stop-over here on a round-the-world trip," proclaimed the *Herald.* Since his previous appearance in 1933, promised the paper, "he has replenished his bag of tricks." Highlighting the Sunday afternoon program was a team race that pitted Mossman's American champions against "a British combine."

Bicycle racing returned to Olympic Park in June 1937, when the Amateur Bicycle League of America sanctioned a card of sprint races on the park's one-fifth mile dirt track. Among the competing pedalers were four members of the 1936 U.S. Olympic team, the 1935 national road champion, Cecil Hursey, and dirt track champions from New York and New Jersey. Featured events included a one-mile race for girls and a junior contest for riders under 16.

Pie eating contests sponsored by Mrs. Wagner's Pies enlivened summer Saturday afternoons throughout the Thirties and Forties. Separate contests were staged for adults and children, with prizes (usually two pies and a small trophy) to the fastest eater, the one who ate the most and the contestant with the messiest face. Close to a thousand blueberry and apple pies were gobbled up by eager eaters each year. Watermelon eating contests were equally popular.

Food of another sort greeted visitors in August 1939 when the New Jersey Baker's Board of Trade held a "monster" bakers day picnic at the park.

Newspaper ads of the Thirties.

Heading up a varied display of bakery products were novelty birthday and wedding cakes containing hidden music boxes that played when the cakes were cut. Participating bakers organized by Henry Dylla and August Betz gave away free admission tickets with each purchase.

Other events during the 1939 season included boxing matches in the ballroom for the benefit of the Underprivileged Kiddies Camp Fund, the annual orphan's outing and, during the Labor Day weekend, the baby contest. One-year-old Donald Wenberg in the guise of Moses in the bullrushes won a $10 first prize in the carriage division.

Featured on local radio and in area nightclubs, Richard Himber's Orchestra enlivened the dance hall on Saturday nights during the late Thirties and early Forties.

The war clouds gathering over Europe and the Far East made everyone jittery as the decade neared end. Olympic Park neighbors were startled as Easter Week 1939 began to see three large military tents go up on the field bordering 40th Street. A score of people called the police, complaining that Bund members were in training at the park. When word of the camp reached the press, a Newark *News* reporter was dispatched to the site to investigate. As he entered the park, he was greeted with a command to "Halt!"

"A little red-headed freckled faced boy shouldering a gun bigger than himself jumped in front of [me]."

"What do you want, he demanded."

"I want to see the man in charge, was [my] reply."

"You can't go in without a guard, said the youth seriously."

"So the reporter, followed closely by the gun with the boy was escorted to a group of older men and the sentry excused himself."

"Was it a Nazi camp? Definitely not. The Irvington Sons of the American Legion are encamping until Sunday in a section of the park. A National Guard cook and members of the senior Legion are with them night and day."

Once home to the Cardinals football team, the field was abandoned in the late Thirties. Charles S. Hausmann, an Irvington funeral director and head of the local Sons of the American Legion, struck a deal with Guenther that allowed the group exclusive use of the field. In turn, the Legion agreed to rehabilitate the fences, gates and turf. "During the years 1938-1941 the field served the S.A.L. well," remembers C. Stewart Hausmann, one of 40 teenagers who took part in the Easter Week camp out. "None of us who enjoyed that week imagined that within a year we would be wearing real uniforms and carrying real guns on the battlefields of World War II."

11

A SIGHT
NOT TO BE MISSED

A daffy entertainment phenomenon that swept the nation during the Depression came to Olympic in late September 1932, when the park's first walkathon opened in the dance hall. Cans of soup and packages of cereal admitted patrons during the first week. Almost a ton and a half of "edibles largely of the canned variety" were turned over to the Community Chest for distribution to the needy, a goodwill gesture that failed to still criticism of what many called a "barbaric spectacle."

Walkathons were the equivalent of a musical endurance contest: Dancers dragged themselves around a ballroom for weeks and sometimes months on end until they collapsed in full view of the paying customers. Dance marathons were roundly condemned as inhumane by the do-gooders, swiftly outlawed in some states but cherished by hordes of fans who came from far and wide to applaud their favorite dancers.

Fifty-eight couples signed up for Olympic Park's marathon, billed to last 3,500 hours. Hailing from such places as California, Florida and Sweden, they all pinned their hungry hopes on winning one of the top cash prizes, which ranged from $500 for the winning couple to $100 for the pair who finished fifth. The prizes were big money in those Depression days, but another attraction was the seven square meals a day guaranteed each contestant.

By mid-December, when they had danced for 2,000 hours, only 11 couples remained on their feet in the yawning ballroom, and on the last day of the event, in late February 1933, there were but five weary survivors—two couples and a single lady who had eliminated her own partner after a heated argument.

But there was to be no prize money awaiting the finalists: On the last day, the promoter, Ed Coronati, skipped town with a reported $2,000 in prize money, $400 contributed by on-lookers and several weeks' wages due the contestants. Stranded without food or lodging, the woebegone dancers were rescued at the eleventh hour when marathon fanciers staged a benefit dance that raised their train fare home. Local police and firemen hustled tickets, Henry Guenther donated the use of the ballroom and Nick Lucas, popular radio entertainer of the era, emceed the program. Three years later, Coronati was nabbed in New York City. Charged with embezzlement, he was returned to Newark where the case was eventually dropped for lack of evidence.

If there was a seamy side to the Olympic Park contest, it wasn't apparent to the thousands of spectators who crammed the ballroom bleacher seats each day and night. According to Danny Hope, a Newark bandleader whose orchestra played the marathon in December, the contest was the biggest attraction in the metropolitan area at the time, with fans bused in from Philadelphia, Trenton, New York and all points between. In the early morning hours, according to Hope, society folk in formal dress would

Marion and Goober Wilson, contestants in the 1935 Marathon, were married later in the show.

Frank and Millie, partners in the W. E. Tebbetts Marathon of 1935.

drop by to cap an evening on the town, occasionally slipping the dancers a cash token for luck. They were frequently joined by area bootleggers, celebrities of a sort in their own right in those days.

Spectators rooted hard for their favorite couple, shouting words of encouragement, passing them cheering notes or tossing floor money. Wild applause filled the hall when a sagging dancer revived just in time to complete a grind. Women in the audience were known to faint dead away whenever a dancer collapsed on the floor from exhaustion. Others collected autographed pictures of the dancers, pasting them in scrapbooks like so many movie stars.

Virtually ignored by local newspapers, which frowned on such bizarre goings-on, the Olympic Park marathon gained wide publicity through daily radio broadcasts of Danny Hope's music on station WAAM. Among the most requested tunes were "Fit as a Fiddle," "Ida," "Linger Awhile," "Sweet Sue," "Muskrat Ramble," "Dream" and the theme song of each broadcast, "Sleep."

Sleep was the most precious commodity in the ballroom. Marathoners were allowed a half hour each day to exercise in the fresh air outside the hall, but otherwise had only 15 minutes out of each hour to attend to personal needs. They slept on cots in a curtained-off area of the room, although even that brief period of privacy was invaded on "cot nights," when spectators were treated to the sight of the male dancers taking their breaks. "When the bell rings," said the *Marathon News*, "the boys will retire. You will see them rush for their cots. Shoes and socks will be discarded and tired heads will fall on the pillows while the music continues to play and the other contestants continue on and on in the dance. If the boys toss in their sleep, you will see them. If

ABOVE — *Danny Hope and his Palais Royal Orchestra entertain at the Coronati Marathon.* BELOW — *A highlight of the 1935 Marathon was this wedding, one of at least two during the show.*

they snore you will hear them. When the siren sends forth its sharp blast, you will see them sleep on and on, paying no attention to the ear-piercing call of the insistent master of the marathon. The trainers will do their duty, tired bodies will be tumbled off the nice resting places to make room for those who are next entitled to the 11 minutes of welcome slumber. It is a sight not to be missed. . . ."

A four-page nickel tabloid published by Coronati, the *Marathon News* touted the Sprints, Five Hour Grinds and Knock-Out Grinds that eliminated all but the sturdiest couples. "It may last one hour, and it may last 20 hours," said the paper of the Knock-Out Grind. "It will certainly be a test of endurance and no one will blame the unlucky kid that falls and brings this terrible grind to a close."

The *Marathon News* ran weekly thumbnail sketches of the contestants packed full of unusual facts. A 19-year-old bathing beauty contestant from Camden, said the paper, drank birch beer, slept in long underwear when marathoning and has "a small mole on her neck and one gold tooth." A former dance hostess bent on becoming an actress "sleeps in pajamas and tosses all night." Fred "Firpo" Bischoff, a 26-year-old ex-prize fighter from Newark who nearly dropped out of the contest when his aged mother

Emcee Red Skelton.

Game contestants from the 1933 Coronati Marathon compete again in a Bicycle Marathon, pedalling stationery bicycles against the clock.

109

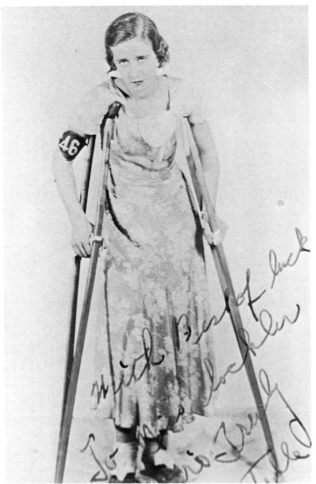

Estelle Johnson was on crutches, her legs bandaged, in the final hours of the 1933 Marathon.

Estelle (above, on a better day) was one of three finalists left high and dry when the promoter skipped town.

was hospitalized, managed to stay in only by walking to the hospital and back accompanied by a judge. One of the rules of marathoning required contestants to be in motion at all times. "He is single," the paper added, "and is not even engaged."

Marathon dances were big money to almost everyone involved but the dancers themselves. General admission on Friday and Saturday nights was a dollar with $1.50 for front-row seats—although seats were cheaper on weekdays and Ladies Nights, when admission was 15 cents. Nurses attended the contestants day and night and a chiropodist was on call to treat their corns and blisters. Vaudeville acts took the stage when the dancers were off the floor.

When the Coronati walkathon ended, 16 of the marathoners, all girls, competed for prize money by pedalling clocked stationery bicycles.

Olympic Park's second dance marathon opened on Jan. 23, 1935, sponsored by W.E. Tebbetts. Lasting four months, the marathon featured a 22-year-old red-headed rubber-faced emcee named Red Skelton who kept up a running patter of jokes, sang songs, took pratfalls and poured soda pop on his head from 8:30p.m. to 2:30a.m. every night. Among Tebbetts' contestants were two others who later gained national fame, June Havoc and Frankie Laine. The 1935 marathon had its share of excitement, including a pair of teenage girls in the audience who tried to commit suicide, one by swallowing iodine, and the nuptials of two of the drowsy couples, performed right before the admiring eyes of the paying customers.

12

PARK PERSONALITIES

History is nothing more nor less than biography on a grand scale. Without "Beefy" Becker, there never would have been an Olympic Park in the first place. Christian Kurz and Herman Schmidt transformed a popular beer garden and picnic grove into a modern amusement park. Henry Guenther guided Olympic's destinies during its glory years. Even today generations of park goers fondly remember Captain Joe and Bubbles.

Few Were So Esteemed, or So Faithful

Following the collapse of the German revolution in 1848-49 tens of thousands of would-be republicans fled their country a step or two ahead of the royal police. Among the "Forty-eighters" seeking freedom in America was John A. Becker (1829-1892), a native of Hanau who crossed the Atlantic with his brother, William, to settle in Newark. A goldsmith of exceptional talent and energy, Becker was general foreman at Carter, Hawkins & Sloane, a jewelry firm that employed some 100 men in its Mulburry Street plant. Becker and his wife, the former Lissette Jardin, moved to Middleville, later known as Hilton and now Maplewood, in 1870.

A prominent member of Newark's German-American community, Becker was one of the founders of the city's Republican Party in the late 1850s. With his fellow goldsmiths he organized the Turnverein, Newark's first athletic society, in 1850. Active in the goldsmiths' Mutual Aid Assn., he was president of the Mutual Homestead Assn. and an enthusiastic member of "Aurora" and "Eintract," two of the oldest and largest of the many German singing societies that flourished in Newark during the second half of the 19th century. "Beefy" Becker, as his friends called him, was a man of comfortable means, ample girth and cheerful disposition who in his later years divided his time between his farm at Middleville and the thousands of visitors who flocked to his beloved "Waldschen" each summer.

Becker died on July 27, 1892, from injuries suffered when he fell from a wagon, survived by his wife and an adopted son, Wilhelm. Burial was in Irvington's Clinton Cemetery. "The ranks of the old-time Germans are thinning faster and faster," lamented the New Jersey *Freie Zeitung* when Becker died. "His death will affect a wide circle of people, for among the oldest generation of Germans few were so esteemed as an honorable man in the fullest sense of that word, or so faithful a member of the many societies to which he belonged."

Every Inch the Perfect Dutchmen

Tall and heavy-set, with his sparse hair cropped short and the sternest of mustaches perched upon his lip, Herman H.A. Schmidt (1860-1929) looked every inch the perfect "Dutchman." He was also a savvy entrepreneur who had made his mark in Newark business circles long before he acquired Becker's Woods in 1904. Schmidt was 12 when his parents left their native Saxony and barely out of school when he joined his father in the charcoal business. By the 1890s, young Herman, now a full partner with his father, was known as "Charcoal Schmidt," a nickname he wore with pride for the remainder of his life. After the charcoal industry went into a decline, Schmidt organized the Standard Birch Beer Co., serving as secretary-treasurer for five years.

Schmidt was an aggressive and occasionally very stubborn businessman who knew intuitively what his park's predominantly German patrons wanted and spared no expense satisfying them. He loved good fun, fine food and "gemutlich" music; until 1912, when he lost his magic touch, he made a great deal of money serving up all three commodities in generous portions. Even as attendance began to fall off, he maintained his own standards. Spending lavishly on the park, he ran up a huge debt of $110,000 by the time his creditors forced him into bankruptcy.

Schmidt, who married Emma Baudistel, and Christian Kurz, husband of Emma's sister, Bertha, got along tolerably well while they were fifty-fifty partners, but after Schmidt lost the park in 1915 and Kurz was brought in as its new manager, an understandable coolness developed between them. His bankruptcy was a heavy blow from which Schmidt never recovered; embittered and much reduced in circumstances, he died at his Irvington home on June 23, 1929, following a heart attack, survived by his wife, a son, Herman, and two daughters, Ida and Clara.

Christian Kurz (1857-1916) was one of Newark's best-known tavern owners of his day. Born in Wurtemberg, Germany, he arrived in Newark when he was 17 and worked as a type-setter and newspaper editor before opening his first saloon on lower Springfield Avenue in the heart of the German district. Several years later, he bought the Old Fashioned on Orange Street, attracting a large and loyal clientele, then managed Bay View Park before opening the Colosseum on Springfield Avenue. He developed the Colosseum (later known as Laurel Garden) into one of Newark's most popular taverns and favorite place of assembly for the city's numerous German societies. The Colosseum's dance hall, lodge rooms, bowling alleys, banquet halls and adjoining tree-shaded beer garden could accommodate nearly 10,000 people. Kurz helped finance his brother-in-law's expansion of

Olympic Park but was content to remain a silent partner, concentrating his efforts instead on the Colosseum, a demanding year-round operation. From 1904 to 1910, when Schmidt and Kurz parted company, the Colosseum doubled as Olympic Park's business and ticket office. Hans Wevers served as general manager of both the park and the Colosseum until 1908.

Several years after he sold out his interest in the park to Schmidt, Kurz disposed of the Colosseum, forced into retirement by ill-health. Kurz returned to Olympic Park in 1915 but poor health dogged his footsteps. As the 1916 season began, the pressures of managing the park and mounting concern over the state of his own health became unbearable. On June 3, 1916, after supper, he went to his room in the family quarters above the park's tavern, took a revolver in hand and committed suicide.

The Brass Band King

When a Newark shoemaker named Clemente Basile and his wife Filippina bought their 8-year-old son a $3 cornet, they hoped he might be a musician someday. Instead, he became America's Brass Band King, one of the best known and most admired bandmasters of his time. Affectionately nicknamed "Mr. Five by Five," the rotund bandleader was to entertain Olympic Park audiences for a record 49 years, playing as he once put it, "everything from mud opera to grand opera."

Joe Basile (1889-1961) stirred crowds with his music from the day in 1902 when he was the featured cornet soloist at a summer band concert in Newark's Branch Brook Park. After a stint at New York City's National Conservatory of Music, he began touring on the Keith vaudeville circuit, billed as the 16-year-old "Boy Wonder." At 19, he joined the brassiest of all bands, Al Sweet's Ringling Brothers Circus Band, playing second trumpet and, at 23, he made his first appearance at Olympic Park as solo trumpet with Baudistel's Dance Orchestra. Ten years later, in 1922, he was hired to lead the park's brass band, a post he would hold for the next 39 years.

Although Olympic Park fans remember him as the roly-poly conductor in the white uniform who led the band concerts and music for the circus, Basile's half-century plus in show business ranged far beyond the park. After 1923, when he formed the Madison Square Garden Band, he played at more circuses, parades, conventions, sporting events and charity affairs than any other bandmaster in America. During his peak years, Basile would play between 25 and 30 state fairs annually and, after Olympic Park closed for the season, he was the regular bandmaster at the New York State Fair, the New Jersey Fair at Trenton and the Allentown and Flemington fairs, both of which featured him for over 30 years. Basile was a one-man musical industry. At one time he maintained a club house in Newark for 200 musicians, with fancy band uniforms for each. During the Thirties and Forties, Basile could suit up a 100-man band on 24 hours notice. It was not unusual for Basile bands to be playing several East Coast engagements on the same day hundreds of miles apart. Affiliated with the Hamid-Morton band circuit for three decades, Basile managed as many as three bands in a single season.

Basile was a musician of prodigious energy despite his impressive bulk. When he wasn't conducting at Olympic Park, the five-foot five-inch tall 272 pound maestro provided music for every occasion, including Italian funerals. The veteran bandleader probably saw more sports events than any other musician of his day. During the 17 years he conducted the Madison Square Garden Band, they played at prizefights, hockey games, skating exhibitions and bicycle races. In 1923, when Jack Dempsey floored the Wild Bull of the Pampas, Basile was the third man in the ring, tooting, "You May Belong to Somebody Else but Tonight You Belong to Me." After that performance, Tex Rickard, the fight promoter, promptly dubbed Captain Joe "The Brass Band King." Basile's bands were a regular feature at the six-day bicycle races at the old Newark Velodrome, at World Series games, football matches and political rallies.

Basile's far-flung activities and continuous travelling would have tired a much younger man, but as Basile grew older he worked harder. When he was 61, he turned TV personality, leading the band on the Sealtest Big Top Circus, a Channel 2 show broadcast from Camden's Convention Hall on Saturday afternoons. Basile led the Big Top band from 1950 to 1957, co-starring with ringmaster Jack Sterling. Among the tunes TV audiences heard were three Basile wrote himself, "Wild Horse Gallop," "Excelsior Tango" and "Amigo Mio."

Basile spent much of his time helping others, especially crippled children. In 1940, he founded the 65-piece Shriners Goodwill Band, entertaining at hospitals, old-age homes and orphanages. On one memorable day, he conducted 1,500 musicians in a Reading, Pa., fund-raiser for crippled children. Shrine hospitals were his favorite charity and he played at most of them, gaining life memberships in 37 Shrine Temples.

Joe Basile was a recognized leader in the music world. In 1953, the industry presented him its Golden Clef Award at ceremonies at Olympic Park marking his golden jubilee. A year earlier, Cornell University had awarded him an honorary doctorate in music.

Basile loved his work—"I've enjoyed every note I ever played," he said once —but he especially enjoyed the children. On his cross-country travels, he would always find time to send scores of postcards to the youngsters he had met in Shrine hospitals. Basile was attending the Shriner's Convention when he died, leading the band in the traditional Rose Bowl parade. The band had just finished playing "Onward Christian Soldiers" when Basile suddenly collapsed and died of a massive heart attack. A sentimentalist who loved life, and who was loved in turn by everyone who knew him, Captain Joe summed up his career a few years before he died when someone asked why he spent so much time giving free hospital concerts. "You get all the rewards you ever need," he replied, "from the faces of the children."

Symbolizing a Show Business Tradition

She is best remembered as Captain Joe Basile's vocalist, but she was much more than that. When the attractive, statuesque blond songstress stepped proudly to the microphone, she symbolized a show business tradition. After a successful career as a trapeze artist ended abruptly in near-tragedy at age 26, she overcame incredible odds to launch a second, more successful career in music. Bubbles Riccardo (b. 1915) lost her arm in that tragic accident but not her courage or her capacity to entertain people. Today, nearly 20 years after her final performance, her name still evokes cherished memories. Park fans have not forgotten those long-ago Sunday afternoon sing-alongs she led in the grove near the bandstand, nor the thrill they experienced when she sang the Star-Spangled Banner as the circus began.

Born Elsie Ashforth, her parents were the famed Flying Riccardos, aerialists who dazzled European crowds before coming to America on the eve of World War I. Here they toured with the Ringling Brothers Circus, then travelled from coast to coast performing at hundreds of state fairs and circuses. The Ashforths were in New York City between engagements when their daughter was born and even before little Bubbles could talk, she was in show business, playing a newborn baby in one of the early silent movies filmed on Long Island.

When she was seven, Bubbles debuted professionally in San Francisco in the play, "Polly of the Circus." Bubbles attended school in California where her parents were busy with movie work, doubling for many of the well-known stars of that era, including Ronald Coleman, Lon Chaney and Vilma Banky. Bubbles herself subbed for Clara Bow when the circus scenes for "Dangerous Curves," a 1929 release, were filmed.

At 14, Bubbles teamed with three young men to form the Aerial Vessas, later dubbed the Three Jacks and a Queen. Their first engagement was at the Hollywood Bowl. Then she joined her parents' aerial act, playing one country fair after another until the afternoon of September 20, 1941, when tragedy struck. It was at the Huntsville, Ala., fair: The Flying Riccardos swung through the air high above the crowd when suddenly a support strap broke, her father lost his grip on her wrist and Bubbles plunged 50 feet to the earth, injuring her head and pelvis and shattering both arms. Later, fitted too tightly with a cast, her left arm had to be amputated. Bubbles returned to her parents' Long Island home after three months in the Huntsville hospital.

Although she lacked formal musical training, Bubbles enjoyed a colorful soprano voice that soon won her a number of radio spots in the New York area. In the spring of 1942, she met Joe Basile, who introduced her to Henry Guenther. Both Basile and Guenther remembered her from her appearances at the park as an aerialist, and they admired her spunk. With Guenther's approval, Basile hired Bubbles as his vocalist, an association that was to last until the park closed its doors 23 years later.

Bubbles, who toured with Basile's band during the park's off-season, married Alfred L. Young in July 1944. She remarried after his death and now lives in retirement in New York State.

A Hero in a Class with Lindbergh and Ruth

The amusement park business, Henry A. Guenther once told a reporter, was like any other business. "We have to satisfy our customers," he explained. "Keep them happy. That's the big thing. Keep them smiling." And for 37 years Guenther did just that, giving his patrons "a little bit of Coney Island, the circus, an old-fashioned beer garden and Monte Carlo rolled into one."

Each season a million or so customers passed through his turnstiles beneath signs that said "Smile" and "Learn to Play." Whether they gasped for breath on the plunging roller coaster or sat quietly in the picnic grove listening to the band music and sipping beer, their smiles were the measure of Guenther's achievement.

Contrary to what many people thought, Guenther (1879-1953) had no show business background and, in fact, didn't get into the amusement park business until the ripe old age of 37. Born to a family of Newark brewers, he began his career at 14 after completing grammar school as an office boy at the Union Brewing Co. Sixteen years later in 1909, he resigned as assistant manager to become superintendent of The Home Brewing Co., makers of "The Beer that Gratifies." In 1919, when he bought Olympic Park, he was an officer and director of the company and one of its largest shareholders.

Guenther became involved in the amusement business almost by accident. When Kurz committed suicide at the start of the 1916 season, Home Brewing's substantial investment in the park was thrown into jeopardy. Guenther and his brother, Anthony, an accountant with the firm, agreed to take over the management temporarily to salvage what they could. Initially his brother was the principal manager, but after the show business bug bit him, Henry Guenther took a larger role in park operations, finally abandoning his comfortable desk job at the Newark brewery on the promise that Home would eventually sell him the park. After 1917, Guenther spent most of his summers at Olympic Park learning how to entertain people. Through trial and error he eventually found the formula for success.

Showmanship, Guenther told the Newark *News* in a 1948 interview, was a matter of giving people what they wanted, a simple enough sounding explanation of a risky business. "Up until a few years ago, I went on every new ride we bought," said Guenther. "I figure that most people enjoy what I do. Mostly it works but sometimes we make mistakes, expensive ones, too. I tried rides that didn't go over and I built stadiums and other useless buildings that had to be torn down. I lost a lot of money but I've learned the business now." Scariness was his "secret formula," said Guenther. The more the customers screamed, the better the ride and the bigger the take. "People want a thrill," Guenther continued, "so we try to bring them a different one each year." So anxious were people for thrills, Guenther told the reporter, that they turned out in droves to try the rides on which there had been accidents or fatalities. Although Guenther continually experimented with new attractions, he never deviated far from his formula of "risky rides and games of chance," which, he said, were the real "gimmicks."

Guenther made Olympic Park a success because he understood and liked people, especially youngsters. The Newark *Sunday Call* ran a glowing account of Guenther's career in July 1931: "As they escape from heat in 4,000,000 gallons of water drawn from an artesian well, Irvington youngsters must regard Henry A. Guenther as a hero in a class with Colonel Lindbergh and Babe Ruth. Mr. Guenther has extended the privilege of using the Olympic Park pool to 4,800 school children. The girls and boys have been presented with membership cards which permit them to enter the park and 'swimming hole' at the cost of 10 cents."

"Those who know Mr. Guenther find his latest move typical. His love for children is one of his outstanding characteristics. On several occasions he might have sold his amusement park at a profit which would permit him to lead an existence of ease. Customers, however, always meet with a refusal that leaves no doubt in their mind concerning his feelings in the matter."

' "This business keeps me young,' he says, 'My friends tell me that I haven't changed in appearance during the last 10 years. They may be flattering me; but I know that I don't feel a bit older than I did a decade ago.'"

"Keeping youngsters happy is but one of his aims. He does his best to restore youth to adults. Two mottoes are prominently displayed at the park. They are: 'Smile' and 'Learn to Play.'"

"Mr. Guenther would be the last man to deny that he is in business to make money. But he is happiest when he is host to under-privileged girls and boys. During the years that he has been operating the park, Mr. Guenther has made so many friends that it is a rare day when he doesn't have several hundred guests."

Long before he became associated with the park, he had given freely of his time to help Newark's youth. In 1902 and 1903, he served as school commissioner, winning election as a Republican in a heavily Irish ward.

For five years, he was a trustee of the Newark City Home for Boys and after that was a director of the Newark Crippled Children's Home. When Newark celebrated its 250th anniversary in 1916, he was chairman of the pageant committee. Active in the Elks, Masons, Junior Order and Shriners, Guenther was the first president of the Irvington Recreation Council. Twice each year he turned the park over to the Elks and Shriners, with admission and all rides free to the thousands of boys and girls who flocked there. Three-Cent Days were inaugurated to open the park to youngsters who might otherwise miss the fun due to lack of money.

Guenther's other interests ranged from politics to banking. He was treasurer of the Essex County G.O.P. and, in 1929, tried unsuccessfully to wrest the county chairmanship from the entrenched machine. During the Twenties and Thirties, he was director of two mortgage guaranty companies and served on the board of directors of five building and loan associations. In 1931, he was president of the Building and Loan Exchange of Essex County. Two years later his peers in the amusement industry elected him president of the National Assn. of Amusement Parks. Guenther and his wife, the former Mary Fuchs, who were married in 1909, had two sons, Henry Jr., born 1911, and Robert, born four years later.

For all his other activities, Olympic Park remained Guenther's first love. Throughout the park his genial but very straight-laced personality dominated. During the season, Guenther was at the park 15 hours a day, overseeing every aspect of the operation. Setting an example for his patrons, he always wore a tie and jacket no matter how hot or humid the weather. He slowed down somewhat in his later years, cutting his workweek to 75 hours and delegating much of the day-to-day responsibilities to his two sons. Guenther died at his Maplewood home on August 24, 1953, a few hundred feet from the park he made famous, within sound of the laughter of his smiling customers.

114

13

THE OLD CROWDS RETURN

America's economy still languished in the doldrums when the Wehrmacht lunged across the Polish frontier in September 1939. But the outbreak of a second European conflict quickly forced the nation to a war-footing: Long-silent plants hummed with activity again, people were at work and, for the first time in a decade, there was plenty of spending money around. The country's entry into the war in December 1941 added more fuel to the economy, now at its strongest since the heady days of the Twenties.

America's new-found prosperity was a godsend to the amusement park industry, which had suffered through the leanest decade in its history. Despite war in Europe and the Pacific, a tremendous exuberance pervaded the country: Americans were proud, confident and glad to be back to work again. The old crowds returned in record-breaking numbers, ready to enjoy the delights so long denied them by slim paychecks.

Olympic Park's attendance broke new records every month. Gas rationing and a shortage of tires drastically curtailed automobile usage, but public transportation continued to roll. Most of the park's regular employees and concessionaires were beyond draft age, although summer help traditionally recruited from high school and college was hard to find. Shortages of all kinds were commonplace. New rides were as scarce as hen's teeth while material to repair the old ones had to be begged or bor-

rowed. European-made souvenirs disappeared from the stands. Nicholas Giuliano's food concessions were the hardest hit. Because many food items were rationed, the stands could open only on a limited schedule. With sugar in limited supply, soda and candy were more expensive when available. Meat rationing forced Giuliano to substitute a pepper and egg concoction for his always-popular roast beef sandwich. Despite all the disruptions, the Forties were good years at Olympic Park.

Uncle Don, WOR's famed kiddie's pal, returned to Olympic Park in June 1940 to head a team of radio personalities raising funds for area underprivileged youngsters. The bill included Bubbles Mandel, a beauty contest winner; Creighton Hagnus, "pocket edition of Fred Astaire;" and Fred Montano, "boy wonder tap dancer." A jitterbug contest and music by Anson Scott's Cottage Club Orchestra rounded out the program, held in the park's new dance hall.

Youngsters still held a special place in Henry Guenther's heart. Lillian Daniels presented a series of eight song and dance shows on the outdoor stage in 1941, featuring a troop of 14 boys and girls between four and 16 years of age. "These supplement the daily free circus and the Thursday night quiz program on the Olympic entertainment calendar," reported the *Herald*.

A beautiful baby contest sponsored by the Daughters of America drew 1,200 entries in July 1941. Three-year old Patricia Young, a chubby brown-eyed

Bobby soxers on their way to the main gate, a typical war scene.

Three balls for 10¢. If you hit the target, a black-face "loudmouth" fell into a tank of water.

A baby pig came squealing down the slide when the target was hit.

116

brunette, copped first prize, a loving cup and gold medal. A month later, the local Polish Council for Relief sponsored another baby parade. Edward Furlong and Barbara Pavlak, both three, were crowned King and Queen.

Ten thousand employees of Newark's Prudential Insurance Co. converged on Olympic Park in July 1942 for the company's annual all-day summer outing. Gasoline rationing forced Prudential to replace its usual seashore excursion with festivities closer to home.

When Olympic opened its 1943 season, the advertising emphasis was on its accessibility—"its portals [are] passed by a dozen bus lines," read the ads. "Normal bus service from much of Essex County, lower Morris County and the more populous sections of Union County carries customers practically to the park gates. Ample vehicles are in operation to avoid crowding and service is frequent." Despite the copywriter's claims, the buses were usually crowded to the bar, especially on weekends when long lines waited to board at the Chancellor Avenue gate for the trip home.

A vast change had come over the park since the war began, noted a reporter who visited in June 1943. "Soldiers monopolizing the shooting gallery for 'busman's holidays,' civilians throwing balls at Japanese crockery and effigies of Hitler, Hirohito and Mussolini, bicyclists pedaling in from the provinces—all are wartime aspects at Olympic Park. . . . With business better than at the same time a year ago, probably because of the park's accessibility by bus from anywhere in North Jersey, the management has been admitting service men and women of all military branches gratuitously to the park and its swimming pool."

"Mrs. Caroline Erth of Brooklyn, operator of the shooting gallery, says uniformed men pepper away at the targets almost to the exclusion of admiring civilians and that 'in my 25 years in this business, I've never seen such accurate marksmanship.' Popular among the park's new features is a throwing game in which the Axis trio, hit in the head with baseballs, lose their trousers. The Red Cross is registering blood donors at a stand in the park, patriotic themes permeate the twice-daily band concerts, family groups bring picnic baskets and avoid trips to distant shore or mountain resorts. A bicycle rack adjoins the spacious parking lot, devoid of all save employees' cars."

The park's empty parking lots were not the only reminders that there was a war on. Victory Gardens sprang up in the old stadium and Joe Basile proudly led his 50-piece band in his own march, "Victory

World War II concessionaires such as Bea Volz substituted Japanese soldiers and German paratroopers as shooting gallery targets.

Parade," at the twice-daily concerts. The park's "thrush," Bubbles Riccardo, trapeze artist turned soprano, sent chills through the crowds with her stirring rendition of the national anthem. Although the government lifted the pleasure driving ban in time for the 1944 season, Guenther urged patrons to use the bus lines to save both gasoline and tires. "The parking lots will be available, however, for those who drive to the amusement center which is only a half gallon of gasoline away from any part of North Jersey."

The 1945 season boasted the highest attendance in 15 years, ranking it with the halcyon days of the Twenties. A Fourth of July crowd of 105,000, many of them attracted by the park's first fireworks display since the war began, was one of the largest single-day gates in the park's history. Shortages still abounded, however, as the nation shifted its energies to the Pacific theatre and the defeat of the Japanese Empire. Reported the local press: "All park concessions are open daily except the shooting gal-

117

Captain Joe Basile

broadcast from Tokyo Bay kept most patrons at home glued to their radios. An eerie quiet befell the park, and the few visitors who arrived were outnumbered by concessionaires and employees.

Henry Guenther's son, Robert, now assuming an active role in the park's management, reported increasing throngs of picnickers in the grove: "It may be nostalgia for the days gone by or it may be a new generation's appreciation of their parent's wisdom in relaxing with a sandwich and a beverage beneath shady trees." Whatever the cause, the Guenthers were pleased as park attendance figures remained high throughout the Forties. Servicemen and women in uniform were admitted free through the end of the 1947 season.

In August 1945, the park announced that no female over the age of 15 would be admitted wearing shorts. Males still had to wear ties and any patron causing a disturbance was unceremoniously ejected by the park's police chief, Artie Kuhn, a former iron

worker who doubled as ticket-taker at the circus. The park's maintenance crew remained hard at work, as usual. Stands and rides were painted each spring, the midways swept each morning and any stray piece of paper hunted down by a staff of 12.

The park's first post-war season formally opened after two weekend previews on May 18, 1946. "Henry Guenther has given his spot a general face-lifting thru use of paint and the addition of several rides," reported *Billboard*. "With the gas buggy trade once more a factor, the parking lot has been doubled in area and paved. New rides are a Cuddle Up, Bubble Bouncer, Helicopter and Auto Speedway. A new Skooter basin, 250 feet long, has been built, and some of the older rides have been shifted to new locations. Ed Ball's Kiddyland has been renovated and has added several attractions."

The '46 season was a musical one, with a birthday salute to George M. Cohan on July 4, a Victor Herbert Day in August and, in between, a guest appear-

lery, where a war-time lack of ammunition precludes continuous operation. The service folk who chiefly patronize the gallery, however, are transferring their attention to the ever-popular games and to a machine gun concession which substitutes water for bullets." The park's annual baby parade, held on Aug. 25, featured a special division for "GI Juniors," children of servicemen.

V-J Day, which marked the end of the war, was one of the worst days in the park's long history, but no one was complaining. The surrender ceremonies

LEFT — *Circus star Clem Billing puts dachshund through paces, August 1949.* RIGHT — *A matinee performance.*
BELOW — *A standing-room-only crowd packs the circus arena during the late Forties.*

The Dobish Daredevils performed in the "Motorcycle Syndrome" during the Thirties. In the Forties Ethel Purtle and her two lions, King and Queenie, spun around the sharply-banked sides of the motorcycle bowl to the delight of thousands.

The Fun House was called Hogan's Alley in the Forties. Near the Pony Track, it featured crooked rooms, rubber hose snakes and hidden air jets. Crowds roared with laughter as ladies climbing the stairs suddenly found their skirts billowing up, lifted by a blast of air. There was a surprise exit slide, too.

ance by the Salaam Temple's 60-piece band led by Captain Basile. The circus continued its two-show a day schedule, with performances at 4 and 9:30p.m. "Daring comedy and the acme of showman's skill" described the show booked for the second week of June, featuring Senora Floradelina, "reputed to be Latin America's most glamorous high wire performer," and the Martel Brothers, "hilarious buffoons on bicycles." Other acts that year included Charles Riano, juggler and clown; Green & Dooley, "the Charlie McCarthy of the open Air;" Rose Mary King, xylophone artist; Kirk's Circus, with the inevitable trained dogs and ponies; the comic caperings of Daisy, "the wonder horse;" and the Tien Tsi Liu Troope, "oriental wonder workers."

The Garden State Flower and Vegetable Show, held Sept. 19 in the ballroom, capped another successful year.

Midgets, motorcyclists and marimba queens shared the circus spotlight in 1948. Hermine's Midgets, a "spectacular" troupe of 30 musicians, dancers, acrobats, clowns, aerialists and athletes, provided the entire show on opening week, replacing the customary four-act bill. In June, the Rob Cimse Company, a European act touring America for the first time, arrived at the park. The "mid-air motor sensations"

rode their motorcycles on the surface of a disc whirling atop a pliant staff. June's audiences were also entertained by Captain Widamen's Baby Elephant, "a petite pachyderm" of unusual talent. "The miniature monster performs tricks few adult elephants have mastered." Other attractions were Reg Kehoe and His Marimba Queens; Montana Kid and his horse, Coley Bay; Oldfield and Ware, "eccentric comedians in a slapstick routine;" and Ross & Ross, "man and woman bag punchers."

An annual park custom was revived in mid-August when Captain Basile's Olympic Park Band played a concert of march music by John Philip Sousa, a tribute to the March King's four spectacular in-person performances at the park in bygone years.

The roller rink was the scene of the first Mass celebrated by parishioners of Saint Paul the Apostle R.C. Church on June 20, 1948. Serving families in Irvington, Maplewood and Union, the fledgling parish worshipped at Olympic Park until September 1949 when its own sanctuary was completed.

Olympic's post-war prosperity continued straight to the end of the Forties and beyond. "Business is booming," Robert Guenther told the press in July 1949. "Attendance has been appreciably greater during the season's first month than it was in the

comparable period in 1948. Weather, a big factor in the amusement business, has been virtually the same for both years. Per capita spending this season is slightly below last year's but grosses are unaffected, with attendance up." Olympic Park took in a reported $700,000 in 1949.

Press Relations Organization, Olympic's advertising agency, said that promotional efforts were much the same in 1948 and 1949, with one exception. Experimental radio advertising in 1948 was dropped in 1949 and the bulk of the promotional budget was restored to newspaper space, the major advertising medium used for more than 30 years.

One reason for Olympic's success was highlighted in a June 1949 *Billboard* magazine survey of American amusement parks that claimed Guenther gave his customers a larger and more costly free entertainment show than any other park in the nation. "Henry A. Guenther, a showman of the old school, insists on four top line acts each week. The standard treat for the customers in most parks is one or at most two free acts." Fittingly, the circus bill for that month included acts of the kind in which Guenther specialized: Veno Berosini, a highwire artist; Jimmy Tracy, a clown on the trapeze; Laine & Crawford, acrobatic contortionists; and The Plutocrats, a dog act.

One of the largest outings ever sponsored by the Newark Lodge of Elks swamped Olympic in early August 1949 when 1,116 Newark children converged on the park, heedless of the 90-degree-plus temperatures. With the unbounded appetite of youth, they devoured 3,500 hot dogs, 2,050 half pints of milk, 175 cases of soda, 4,500 pieces of candy and 1,600 cups of ice cream.

"And if that wasn't enough to send anybody looking for a nice shady spot," claimed the Newark *News*, "the children exuberantly monopolized 24 rides in the park—three were out of bounds. . . . Most of the children, including charges of five Newark orphan homes, 352 crippled children and 129 underprivileged children, all free to roam the

TOP — *During the war years a shortage of meat made stands like this one popular.* MIDDLE — *Bobby Ball gets ready for the Baby Parade. His father, Ed, owned Kiddieland and other concessions.* BOTTOM — *George "Sunshine" Mullins stands behind the counter.* RIGHT, TOP — *Susie Zignoli, Norma McVean and Trudy Krucks are winners of a 1949 pie-eating contest.* RIGHT, BOTTOM — *Dominic Monachio and Betty Ann Budd devour watermelons in 1949 contest.*

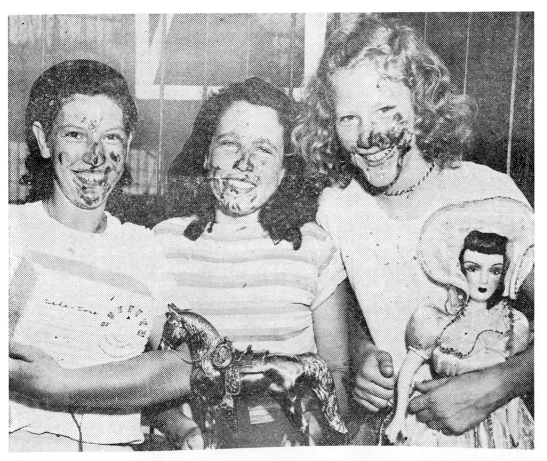

Kiddieland, about 1950, owned and operated by Ed Ball.

Coleen Hector outside Kiddieland, clutching a paper parasol she just won.

Baby Parade Queen Mary Lou Kern strikes a regal pose in the garden area of the goat ride owned by her parents.

Raymond Burke, Charles Pribulick, Barbara Burke and John Pribulick enjoy the Baltimore & Ohio at Kiddieland, 1952.

park at will, rode not once, but many times on the amusements. One 7-year-old boy happily reported that he had ridden the miniature train 19 times."

The children were transported to the park early in the morning in 16 chartered buses. Two doctors, four nurses and an ambulance stood by just in case. Ruled out of bounds were the roller coaster and flying planes, considered too dangerous for the children, and the pony ride, considered too dangerous for the ponies.

The youngster who spent half the day on the miniature train enjoyed Olympic's newest attraction, the "Northern Pacific." Owned by Ed Ball, the ride made its inaugural run in May 1949. A 3,800-pound internal combustion engine hauled 12 open cars with seats for 96 adults or 144 children. "Designed primarily for the small fry, it will be available to them when all the grownups are tired of riding," reported the local press. "Contrary to all expectations, the trade has come from the adults, with only a sprinkling of children so far. . . . The streamliner never

heads for the wide open spaces—a purring gliding ride of nearly a mile—without a full load. The station is a model of comfort and convenience and no railroad offers a pleasanter tour through the hinterland. And it's as wreck-proof as a road can be."

When "Big Top," television's first circus show, debuted in early July 1940, it featured Captain Basile's band and nine acts, every one of which had already appeared at Olympic during the past two seasons. "The Essex amusement park's management retained its four act show. . .all during the years theater-goers were moaning vaudeville was dead," commented one newspaper. "And the top performers today in theater and on television are largely old favorites of Olympic patrons." Added the reporter: "With all its modern rides and amusement devices, Olympic Park always has found the features accompanied by a bit of nostalgia more than holding their own in popularity. Obvious examples are the ferris wheel, the lavish picnic tables under shady trees, games of checkers, the miniature golf course, playground swings for children and the roller coaster."

An assortment of American heroes (plus a few dastardly villains as well) made their appearance at the park in 1950 when the wax museum reopened next to the restaurant.

A savage storm with gusts as high as 108 miles per hour struck the state on Nov. 25, 1950, leaving 22 dead and damage in the millions. At the peak of the storm, winds of gale force uprooted trees, ripped signs from their moorings, stripped masonry from buildings, tore roofs from houses, blew in windows and overturned cars and trucks. Four hundred thousand homes were left without power. The hurricane caused widespread damage at Olympic Park, wrecking the Chancellor Avenue entrance gate, flooding the skating rink, lifting roofs off scores of concession stands and knocking down trees. Hardest hit was the roller coaster, half of which collapsed before the ferocious onslaught. Damage to the park was estimated at more than $125,000.

When the park opened for the 1951 season, visitors were greeted by an entirely new "rollie" built at a cost of $100,000 by the Philadelphia Toboggan Co. "Higher! Safer! Faster!" proclaimed the ads. The roller coaster, said Guenther, had been "redesigned for swifter, more thrilling rides [and] rebuilt for increased safety and greater fun." Otherwise, the park wore its traditional garb. The circus was free, the pool water so clean it was "safe to drink" and the annual baby parade still the best way yet invented for proud parents to brag without offending. The parade of toddlers, accompanied by Captain Joe's band, wended its way around the picnic grove and past the reviewing stand just as it had for more than three decades.

One of Hollywood's "biggest" stars made his New Jersey debut in August. Ferdinand the Bull, at 1,500 pounds the largest trained animal in the entertainment world, grunted his way through two shows daily to the delight of thousands. Gentle Ferdinand, the original model for the Walt Disney movie, was filmdom's biggest ham, claimed his trainer. The bull,

Letty Beardsley, June Simon and Lois Simon "play" basketball, 1950.

June Sonnabend Schwartz spins the wheel at her parents' radio stand, c. 1950.

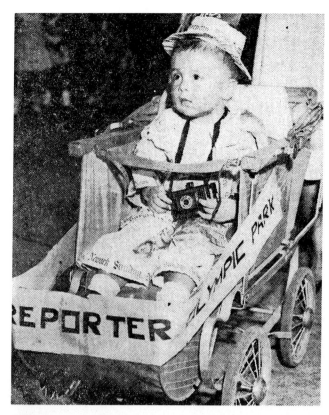

ABOVE — *Gussy Johnson, 3, portrays a newspaper reporter in the 1949 Baby Parade. BELOW — Raymond and Barbara Burke and John and Charles Pribulick at Kiddieland, 1952.*

ABOVE — *The Baby Parade passes the Twister, 1950. BELOW — 1947 Baby Parade Queen Mary Lou Kern on her golden throne, with Lois Simon, a park employee, dressed as a clown.*

The Moon Rocket, Olympic Park, N. J.

ABOVE — *The Moon Rocket, a popular ride whose cars spun around a table tilted at 30 degrees.* BELOW — *A view from the ramp, with the boat ride and Octopus in the foreground; Skee Ball, 40th St. entrance, flying airplanes and haunted castle in the background.*

ABOVE — *Henry Guenther Sr. oversees the 1950 Baby Parade* (right, with megaphone), *while Henry Guenther III leads the pony past the Merry-Go-Round.* BELOW — *The Dude Ranch, owned by Charles Simon. At right rear, the roller rink.*

a 13-year veteran of the footlights, "bows deeply for applause and seems to have an uncanny knowledge of music." Ferdinand returned to the park in 1952, sharing the free circus stage with an assortment of aerialists, trained dogs, somersaulting motorcyclists and jugglers.

Although competition from America's newest entertainment medium would soon affect every amusement park, television was still regarded as something of a fad when Guenther inaugurated Tele-Theater during opening week in 1952. Seven large sets, each tuned to one of the seven New York area stations, were in operation continuously day and night. "Television Theater, Olympic Park's nationally heralded experiment, continues to attract interest among park patrons anxious to see their favorite video programs and still enjoy the park's amusements," reported the press in mid-summer. Although admission was free, television hall failed to catch on

with the public and closed in August 1953.

A drive to rid Irvington of gambling "in all its forms" initiated by Public Safety Director J. Elmer Hausmann in August 1950 dealt the park a heavy blow from which it never fully recovered. Olympic's games of chance, 19 in all, accounted for about 40 percent of the park's business, according to management estimates. The wheels of chance, like all other concessions, had been run honestly ever since they were first installed over 30 years before. Angelo Giuliano, who worked with his father, Nicholas, vividly recalls how Henry Guenther policed his concessionaires. If a patron claimed he was cheated, Guenther took him back to the stand where he told the patron to pick out any prize he wanted. No operator, said Giuliano, ever protested.

In August 1950, Hausmann warned Guenther that all chance wheels had to be eliminated by the end of the season. When the park re-opened in May 1950, with the wheels still in operation, Hausmann threatened a police raid if his order were ignored any longer. "We want to obey the law." said Guenther, who removed the wheels during the first week of June. "We will have nothing at Olympic Park that violates any ruling that is laid down." Maplewood officials, who had also looked the other way for years, had no choice but to enforce the state's anti-gambling laws in their half of the park as well after Irvington acted.

Hausmann struck again three weeks later when a new engineering survey confirmed that 10 pinball machines in the Penny Palace, operated by Milton Brooke, were in Irvington instead of Maplewood. A squad of Irvington police with a large moving van pulled up to the arcade on June 22 to haul off the bagatelle machines from the Irvington side of the stand. Machines on the Maplewood side remained in operation.

Park concessionaires, dismayed by Hausmann's moves, reacted to removal of the chance wheels by

The Ferris Wheel, new in 1950, operated by Dan Peterson for many years.

ABOVE — *The Alaska stand in the grove near the bandstand featured chocolate-covered bananas.* BELOW — *The Northern Pacific was said to be the longest kiddie train ride in the nation.*

Allen K. Harris was one of nine proprietors of Stop and Go games who resumed business on July 24, 1952, after a court restrained Irvington police from interfering with the games.

substituting individual spindles for each player. Use of the spindles, they claimed, required skill; the element of chance necessary to a gambling device had been eliminated. When the police commissioner ordered the spindles removed, concessionaires set up ball-throwing and tossing games instead.

Olympic's concessionaires were angered by Irvington's new-found morality and so was Guenther, who knew that attendance and profits would be badly hurt. Publicly Guenther reacted calmly: "I hold no malice toward Mr. Hausmann," he told a reporter. "I believe he is an honest man, trying to do what he thinks is right." Word that he and his two sons planned to sell the grounds for a housing project were "just so much rumor," smiled Guenther, who admitted receiving a million dollar offer for the park from a real estate broker. Guenther, wrote the reporter, "glanced about the vast expanse of brightly-lighted stands, the new $9,000 Ferris Wheel, the roller coaster that is costing $100,000 to repair hurricane damage and said, 'No, I want to keep my

park. And I want my sons to have it after I retire.'"

Commissioner Hausmann saw red when Olympic Park opened for the 1952 season with nine new Stop and Go machines installed where the wheels of chance had been. Featuring a large numbered board with lights, the machines could be played by 16 patrons at a time who pushed buttons to stop the machine at what they guessed was the winning number. Nearly as popular as the old wheels, the Stop and Go concessions drew large crowds that grew even larger when Irvington officialdom threatened to close them down as well. A restraining order issued by the Superior Court prevented interference with the games until the issue could be litigated.

Stop and Go had its day in court in late January 1953. After a college mathematics professor testified that the game involved both mental and physical dexterity, the court permanently enjoined Hausmann and the Irvington police chief, telling them to leave the games alone. "Good clean fun," said one observer, "has triumphed over bureaucracy."

14

STEAM IN THE STRAIGHTAWAY

Roller skating was one of Olympic's most enduring attractions. During the Twenties and Thirties, the roller rink was open every evening except Mondays, with admission, including skate rental, pegged at 40 cents. Roland Cioni, a professional skating champion from 1914 to 1932, promoted well-attended amateur skating races at the park on Saturday nights.

Roller skating was all the rage during the Forties and Fifties, when nearly a score of clubs enjoyed Olympic's rink. Most active were the Midnight Rollers, Paragon Rollers, Olympian Gliders, Columbia Rollers, Sapphire Rollers, Camptown Rollers, Royal Cadets, Rhythm Rollers, Marite Rollers, Rolleteers, Dreamland Bears, Top Hat Rollers, Patriot Rollers and the Two Tone Rollers.

Skaters from throughout the state were drawn to Olympic's rink by its friendly, club-like atmosphere. "It was like a big family," says Connie Strano Burghardt, who edited a newsletter called the "Dog House" during the waning months of World War II that kept members of the "family" on farflung battlefronts informed about rink activities. The five cent newsletter, a project of the Dog Tag Rollers, contained news of servicemen and special events at the rink. A gossip column that listed who was skating most often with whom may have been its most ardently read feature.

More than a few "pairs" made it a permanent arrangement. Lila Grundfast and Walter Bordens, for example, who saved two well-preserved issues of the "Dog House" for posterity, were listed in the July 1945 copy as "doing more than all right." Another issue that year included the names of Howard Trost, then a Seaman 2/C, and Helen Hartman, who ultimately married, and Robert (later to be Irvington Mayor) Miller and his wife-to-be, Marian Heinrich.

Supplying the organ music for these and other skaters during the Forties was the popular Eddie Baatz, who came to the Olympic rink in 1939 after playing at a number of movie theatres, including the Castle and Sanford. A man of boundless good humor and a fine musician to boot, Baatz operated in a glass-enclosed booth that dominated the south end of the rink. He delighted in answering requests— songs of the era like "Sentimental Journey," "Maybe," "The Hut-Sut Song," "You and I," "The Reluctant Dragon," "Together" and "Boogilie-Woogilie Piggy." Baatz, who played daily from 7:30p.m. to 11:30p.m., also led a 15-piece orchestra in his spare time.

Baatz left Olympic in late 1945 to play at the popular Promenade Cocktail Bar in Newark. Taking his place in the glass booth was Mrs. Mabel Foscato, a veteran of the roller rinks at Paramus and Florham Park.

Another publication devoted to roller skating events at Olympic Park was "Rink News," which appeared in the early Forties. It was published by Barney Williams and edited by Warren Schimunek, sold for a nickel and claimed a circulation of 4,000.

The Marite Rollers, seen here during the early war years, skated at the park from 1940 to 1950. Their name derived from their maroon and white uniforms.

Eddie Baatz was the jovial rink organist from 1939 to 1945.

Lillian Tafaro, a rink regular in the Forties, poses for the photographer.

George Beach commanded the organ booth during the Fifties.

A tattered and yellowing Aug. 5, 1941, issue proclaimed special ticket prices for skating sessions, which ran nightly from 7:30 to 11:30 and on Saturday and Sunday afternoons from 2 to 5. A rink club formed by the management offered discount rates to members who paid a dollar a year fee. Monday and Wednesday were club nights when members could skate for 25 cents. On other nights the cost was 35 cents. Management made it easy for people to join: The dollar fee could be paid in installments—50 cents with the application and 50 cents before six months were up.

In an editorial "Rink News" warned of a crackdown on "public nuisances." The management, it said, "will not allow any petting or mushing in this rink. You will be told once to stop and the second time you will be told to take off your skates and leave the building. The same goes for wheelbarrel skating. . . ." Also targeted were speedsters "who scoot in here, dodge out there and put on the steam in the straightaway."

Park employees helped support "Rink News" with small ads. One was from the floor staff: Floor Manager Johnny Krako, Instructors Fred Butler, Harold Faulks, Edward Paff, Joe Phillips, Inky Dippel, Dot Cohen and Norman Frey and Doorman Milton May. Another was from Head Bartender Jack Vollin and "the rest of the boys who serve that good old brew," Fred Cook, Henry Scheid and Pete Albers. Park policemen Artie Kuhn, Charlie Albert, Phil Bradsley, Frank Harrington, Herman Schmidt, Larry Krampert, Paul Perger and Bob White advertised their good wishes.

When the war began, many of Olympic's young skaters hung up their wheels for the duration. The park's rink was never far from their thoughts, however. "I've been in the Pacific for quite a while now," wrote Fireman 1/C John Swierat in 1945, after receiving a copy of the "Dog House," "and when we men get together and talk of different things, all I've talked about was the Olympic Rink, and of all the friends and the good times I've had there."

The rink's first post-war season opened in December 1945 under the direction of Jack Edelstein, a discharged veteran. During the early Fifties, an old favorite returned to the rink when George Beach, who worked as ticket collector in 1944-45, took over as organist. Beach, a typewriter repairman, was a great favorite of the youngsters. Rarely would a day go by without some young person joining Beach in the glass booth to try his or her hand at the organ. Head guard at the rink in the mid-Fifties was Jack Mendelsohn, whose team of five men enforced the rules against excessive speed, roughhousing and unseemly conduct. Mendelsohn's crew was also on hand to pick up skaters who tumbled to the floor or help the injured to the nearby first aid station.

"Sunday afternoon sessions were by far the best attended," recalls Mendelsohn, "with 300 to 350 skaters jamming into the rink. At times so many came that real skating was out of the question, but everyone had a good time nonetheless. Friday nights were popular with the teenagers, especially the girls who sported short skirts and tied colored pom-poms on their skates. Moonlight skating, when everyone strapped small battery-operated lights on the tips of their skates, was another favorite. Mom and Pop Robbins, who ran the check room and skate repair shop, were there as long as I can remember."

Serious skaters, some of whom paid as much as $100 for a pair of precision wheels, patronized the rink on weeknights when it was less crowded. During the summer, a prefabricated racing rink was set up for them on the Chancellor Avenue side of the building. The 20-member Olympic Skating Club's racing squad, organized in 1956 by Ralph Antrosiglio, competed in the Penn-Jersey League, racing every two weeks. Outfitted in their navy and powder blue racing togs, the team racked up high scores in the standard two-mile and 26-mile marathon races sponsored by the league.

The Jack Rabbitt *viewed from the lower Midway, c.1940.*

No American amusement park of any size is without its roller coaster, and Olympic Park was no exception. Although the cost of maintenance and insurance was steep, Olympic's coaster was always its biggest attraction and best money-maker.

Herman Schmidt understood a coaster's drawing power early on, erecting an exciting ride less than five years after he opened his new playland. Henry Guenther tore down Schmidt's coaster in 1926, replacing it with a much larger affair designed by John A. Miller and George Baker for the Philadelphia Toboggan Co., which built it at a cost of nearly $50,000. Covering an area 325 by 200 feet, the *Jack Rabbit* was remodelled in 1937.

After the hurricane of November 1950 toppled large sections of the coaster, the Guenthers hoped to rebuild using about two-fifths of the original. But when construction began they found that the entire ride had to be replaced for reasons of safety. Built by the Philadelphia Toboggan Co., Olympic's new roller coaster went into operation in mid-July 1951 with a price tag of $100,000.

The Jet, similar in style to its predecessor but "higher, safer and faster," enjoyed the same phenomenal success. Although expensive—a ticket cost 40 cents in the Fifties and a dollar in the Sixties—for many patrons it was the best ride in the park. Operators encouraged the loudest screamers to take a second ride free, a gimmick that never failed to attract even more patrons. Both the *Jack Rabbit* and *The Jet* were owned by Olympic Park, Inc., the Guenther family corporation.

Inspected weekly by the insurance company and daily by Guenther's staff, Olympic's coaster was among the park's safest rides. Fatalities in 1921, 1929, 1949 and 1963 were attributed to patron misconduct.

Writing in *Roller Coaster Fever*, coaster expert John Waldrop called *The Jet* a medium-sized compact ride "that pulled a punch on nearly every drop it traversed." It had several good swoop turns, added Waldrop, and was "well-paced." John Allen, a coaster designer for the Philadelphia Toboggan Co., once described Olympic's roller coaster as "the best that was ever built for its size." *The Jet* was demolished in August 1969.

ABOVE, LEFT — *All aboard for a breathtaking trip.* ABOVE, RIGHT — *Screamers enjoyed a second ride free.*
BELOW — *After the November 1950 hurricane the roller coaster was a jumbled heap of splintered lumber.*

ABOVE — Liberty *in all her glory.* BELOW, LEFT — *A close-up of one of the horses.* BELOW, RIGHT — *A triumph of the carver's art by Daniel C. Mueller.*

Photos from "A Pictorial History of the Carousel" courtesy Frederick Fried.

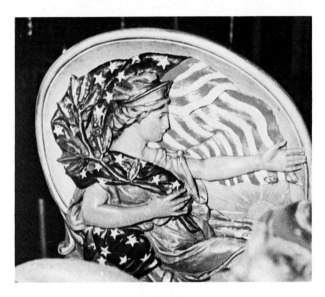

She may well have been the largest merry-go-round ever built in America, and surely she was magnificent. A product of a proud and ancient art, she was elaborately decorated in red, white and blue, with shields, eagles, flags, Miss Liberty herself, Roman chariots, extravagant sleighs, prancing horses and scenes of the American countryside. *Liberty* was Olympic Park's most popular ride, and the best-loved of them all.

Liberty was originally created in 1914 by the Philadelphia Toboggan Co. for Belle Isle Park, Detroit. Returned to her Philadelphia birthplace and rehabilitated in 1928, she was acquired by Henry Guenther and installed at Olympic Park in 1929 to reign for 37 seasons, a delight to millions.

Illuminated by 3,000 lights, *Liberty* had a 60-foot platform, 80 wooden horses, four chariots and sleighs and seated 99 passengers five abreast. Daniel C. Mueller, one of America's premier artists, carved many of the horses and chariot boards. Other craftsmen, mainly German and Italian-born, created the elaborate outer and inner facings, colorful chariots and sleighs and unusually graceful steeds at Philadelphia Toboggan Co.'s Germantown factory. *Liberty*'s horses were triumphs of the woodcarvers art: One carried a shoulder festoon of roses; another's haunches support a quiver of Indian arrows, while the likeness of Eric the Red covered another's flank. Even a baby lamb lying behind the saddle was carved into the maple back of one horse.

A band organ imported from Italy provided *Liberty*'s music. Heavily decorated with gold leaf, the band organ featured a cymbel, bass drum, snare drum and four graceful carved dancers who twirled to the sound of music. Tiny doors opened and closed to control the volume of the pipes concealed behind the facade. Stirring marches and popular tunes of the early part of the century spilled from the paper music rolls, adding a magic touch for the riders gliding effortlessly on the "spinning lady."

After the park closed *Liberty* was shipped to California, redesigned by Walt Disney artists and installed as the center-piece of a medieval courtyard in Fantasyland, Walt Disney World, Orlando, Florida. Rechristened Cinderella's Golden Carrousel, *Liberty* continues to thrill riders just as she did at Olympic Park for so many years.

15

YIELDING AT LAST

Henry Guenther's death in August cast a heavy pall over the remainder of the 1953 season. Concessionaires, employees and patrons alike felt the loss of the man whose name was synonymous with the park, whose cheerful personality dominated the landmark he built. Although everyone knew "the old man" could never be replaced, the park family carried on in his tradition.

Guenther's son, Robert, became president of the family corporation, his brother, Henry Jr., manager of the park. Later, Robert Jr. was named treasurer and his cousin, Henry III, secretary of the business. Robert, only 38 when he assumed the reins, had grown up at Olympic, making his debut as a Dutch boy in one of the Aborn Opera Co. operettas. A relief cashier at suppertime when he was 12, Guenther became a summer regular after that, working at the park while attending Princeton University and Rutgers University from which he graduated in 1937. Married to the former Elizabeth Gant of Irvington, the World War II veteran was the father of two boys, Robert and William.

New Jersey's largest and oldest amusement park opened for the 1954 season on May 14. A family of high wire artists, the Coronatis, headlined a four-act circus that included a comic juggler, Ted Lester playing miniature musical instruments, and Leon and Eleana's Trained Danes, the inevitable but thoroughly enjoyable dog act.

The Skee Ball concession, just south of the Tumble Bug, was now operated by the Olympic Park corporation. Guenther added 12 machines to the eight that had been there for years, changed from cigarette prizes to flashy merchandise and upped the cost to a dime, a highly successful move other parks soon emulated. Walter Florimont ran the Skee Ball concession in later years.

Robert Guenther was confident the park would benefit from the newly-completed Garden State Parkway. "Our location is only a few blocks away from parkway exits," he said at mid-summer, "and this proximity makes us only minutes away from Bergen, Passaic, Union and Middlesex Counties." Trained elephants, continuous band music and fireworks on the Labor Day weekend brought the season to a close with the largest crowd of the summer.

The nation's only amusement park to offer a free four-act circus began 1955 with Hawthorn's troupe of performing bears. "For the children it will be one of the season's highlights because of their fondness for the brutes. Only seals command as much juvenile interest." In July, Billy Cutten, the Diving Sensation, amazed crowds by diving, ablaze, 100 feet into a flaming tank of shallow water. A week later, The Great Veno, whose "walk of death" made some spectators faint the year before, returned to Olympic Park. "Audiences cringe as Veno seems to fall while he shuffles along a tight wire 100 feet high, his head encased in a sack and baskets on his feet," said the *Herald.* "He is a member of the Berosini family,

Robert A. Guenther

famed in circuses for generations. He hasn't faltered on the fall yet; but he'd only have to miss once."

A mid-summer concert in memory of Victor Herbert featured the park's two stalwarts, Joe Basile, who tootled "Thine Alone" on his silver trumpet, and Bubbles Riccardo warbling "A Kiss in the Dark."

Olympic Park had something for everyone, including two anonymous eight-year old boys from Newark who made the headlines in August 1955. "It all began," went the newspaper story, "when one of the youngsters poked around his mother's bureau and came across $25. Excitedly, he called one of his friends and the two took off for Olympic Park for the gorgeous dream of young boys everywhere—a day at the amusement park with no limitations on wants or money."

"They went on rides—ate to their stomach's discontent—and played all the games they wanted, winning a virtual load of prizes—water pistols—another toy gun—jumping beans—a Howdy Doody toy—a baseball—plastic boats—two small glasses. Oh, what a time they had until they were spotted by Special Officers Smith and Kuhn who couldn't figure out where two unchaperoned boys could get the cash for their flight to fancy. So the boys were taken to police headquarters and the lad with the money

One of Olympic Park's shady walks, c. 1950. The Penny Arcade is at the left with its steam shovels, postcard machines and photo booth.

141

ABOVE — *The picnic grove, c. 1952, with the roller rink at the rear. The bandstand is just out of view at the right.*
BELOW — *Kiddieland, for the 3-to-10 crowd. Barely visible is the famous white elephant.*

had his mother called in."

"All in all, the boys spent only $4.60. But in this day and age—at least to a couple of kids in Olympic Park—$4.60 goes a long way. Pinocchio himself didn't have a gayer time at Pleasure Island."

The two boys from Newark fell victim to a long-standing park policy that required concessionaires and ride operators to report free-spending children to park police. The Guenthers expected customers to be treated fairly; concessionaires and employees who broke the rules were soon gone from the scene.

"We were almost like a family ourselves," remembers one park concessionaire, "and we all worked together to keep Olympic a place of wholesome family entertainment." Angelo Giuliano, who started at the park in 1936 selling hot dogs and hamburgers for a dime each, was a member of one of the park's best known families. His father, Nicholas, first worked at Olympic in 1915 parking horses and wagons. In 1931, he and James F. Caffrey formed a partnership that operated all food concessions until the park closed. Angelo's sister, Lena, handled the payroll.

Business was slow during the Thirties, recalls Angelo, when patrons brought their own lunches, but it boomed in the Forties and Fifties. On a typical good-weather weekend, 900 pounds of hot dogs, 500 pounds of hamburgers and 300 pounds of roast beef would be sold. Anywhere from 30 to 50 part-timers worked the stands, where a roast beef sandwich swimming in rich brown gravy—a Giuliano specialty—sold for 10 cents. Hires root beer was five cents a glass, peanuts a nickel a bag. A stand near the pool sold pizza pies, French fries, hot soup and sandwiches.

Park patrons could always count on a wide variety of mouth-watering, waist-widening refreshments. Popcorn, soda, cotton candy, frozen bananas on a stick, Alaskas, caramels, chocolate-covered bananas, candy, ice cream, fudge and waffles were available. Andrew Peters, who owned a sweet shop in Irvington Centre, ran Candy Land from 1930 until Olympic closed. During the Forties and early Fifties a three-block long line snaking toward Peters' waffle stand was not unusual.

"Swim or play," said a 1952 brochure, "relax comfortably at the circus, enjoy a lunch or a meal in the tree-shaded outdoors, loll in the sun, watch the delight of children, listen to good music. . . ."

The Midway from the Tumble Bug, with the Haunted Castle at left, archery and Moon Rocket at right.

Olympic's concessionaires played a vital role in the park's success. Some, like Julius Schwartz, who operated a number of Stop and Go games, and Edward T. Ball, were fixtures for decades. Ed Ball, who ran the Arcade, Stuffed Cat, Walking Charlie and several Stop and Go games, was at Olympic as long as anyone could remember. Others included Walter Florimont (20-alley Skee Ball and Stop and Go Flasher), Mike Gargiulo (Basketball), George Rochedieu (Fruit Stand), Jim McWilliams (Fish Pond and Kitchenware), Walter Zolkiewicz (Stop and Go), Mel Lawrence (Metro Derby Horse Race), Grace Masapoli (Candy Land Stop and Go) and Sam and Madeline DeVingo (New Hoople Ring Toss).

Barely was the 1956 season underway when the New Jersey Supreme Court ruled that games of chance played for prizes were illegal even if the element of player skill was involved. By the next day more than three dozen games of chance at Olympic Park were shut down tight, as were games at Palisades Park in Fort Lee and along the New Jersey Shore. The court ruling had an immediate and devastating effect on the park, with attendance plummeting to its lowest level in years. Concessionaires laid off employees and tried to sell their stock, none too successfully. "The statute the Supreme Court cited is 60 years old," complained concessionaire Tony D'Auria. "I didn't even know it was on the books!" A last-minute effort by the State Legislature to overturn the top court's ruling died on the gover-

nor's desk. Skill games were to remain closed for the next four seasons.

A Herschell-built Twister ride installed for the 1956 season was christened "Rock 'n Roll" to avoid confusion with one of Olympic most popular attractions, a dark ride called the Twister.

Olympic park sported a new look in 1957. With the lucrative skill games banned, Robert Guenther decided to use some of the empty stands for advertising. Public Service Electric and Gas, the N.J. Commission for the Blind and the Chamber of Commerce rented space. Other stands were torn down. Guenther refused to follow the lead of Palisades Park, which sold dolls, toys, jewelry and appliances at the stands once occupied by the games. "We can't hope to compete with the highway stores in the sale of general merchandise," said Guenther. Surprisingly, the number of concessionaires who decided to carry on was far higher than expected. Of the 39 categories of games affected by the ban, less than half decided to call it quits. Instead, they revised the games, offering gifts of equal value for all players. Professor Baker, the weight-guesser, whose stand was near the ramp, paid off whether he nailed down a patron's poundage or not. Olympic concessionaires admitted the new games were lack-luster versions of the old skill games, and doubted their pulling power. "We'll try to get along," said one. "Whatever we take in is better than nothing. And

Laughing Sam, in front of the Twister next to Kiddieland. Dressed like a hayseed, Sam laughed up a storm. One of the laughs was that of Henry Guenther Jr.

who knows, maybe someday things will be the way they used to be."

Olympic Park added a new helicopter ride and a machine gun gallery to try to make up for the revenue lost when the games closed. Although neither Robert nor Henry Guenther would estimate the loss, they admitted it was "sizable."

While the ban on skill games lasted, rumors increased that the park would be closed. In 1958, word had it that the park would be sold for a mammoth housing development, including high-rise apartments and a shopping center. "This is about the 25th time something has come up since Dad died," said an exasperated Henry Guenther. "Let's put it this way; we've set a price and it hasn't been met yet." According to the press, the owners were looking for $5 million for the 40-acre tract. Skill games returned to Olympic Park in time for the 1960 season after voters in both Irvington and Maplewood approved a statewide referendum legalizing them in November 1959.

The unparalleled success of Disneyland, which opened in 1955, introduced a new element in the amusement business. Theme parks, as Disneyland and its progeny came to be known, offered stiff competition for the public's entertainment dollar. Many traditional parks, some as old as Olympic, poured millions into new rides and attractions; others closed their doors. In contrast, Olympic Park changed little during the late Fifties and early Sixties. Although attendance gradually slipped and costs were up, concessionaires still made a respectable profit. The Guenthers were not about to invest heavily in the park and made no bones about their willingness to sell when the right offer came along. Until then, but only until then, the park would remain in operation.

The growing Civil Rights movement forced a change in policy in the mid-Fifties, when Blacks were admitted. Before that, it had been common knowledge that Blacks were not welcome and few had ever sought entry.

Opening with the Essex County preliminaries to the Miss Universe Contest, the 1957 season swung into full gear when Zacchini, the Human Cannonball, was shot from a cannon across the circus arena and into a net—"when all goes well." In June, 500 orphans visited the park as guests of the Elks. The pool had been spruced up, with a new restaurant and an amusement arcade and, in July, Zeke Manners and his Rock-Billies, radio and TV celebrities, made an appearance.

Olympic Park was the site of the 1959 State Championship of the "Laff Olympics," sponsored by something called the National Laugh Foundation. "Individual laughers, and Laff Teams through-

BELOW — *The park's bandstand and picnic grove after a winter snowstorm.*

A group of handicapped and underprivileged children enjoy a boat ride during the Newark Elks' annual outing, August 1959.

out the state have been invited to participate in the competition to find the most versatile, talented and charming laughers in the Men's, Women's and Children's Laff Competition," reported the press. "Laughters are required to do three types of laughs—the giggle, the robust-roar and the harmonious. Then they are allowed to do three of their own to show their versatility." Scoring was on the basis of ingenuity, individuality and projection by judges selected by the National Laugh Foundation. Winners of the Championship in 1959, said the paper, would be eligible for the International Laugh Year Laff Olympics scheduled for 1960.

Art Ford's "Teen Stand," a popular record and interview show broadcast weekday afternoons over WNTA-TV, brought its cameras to Olympic Park for the 1959 season. Highlighting the show was Ford's salute to top high schools in the area, with profiles of student activities as well as their taste in popular music. The old Skillo building, unused since 1957, was revamped with a large dance floor and benches for the teenagers.

Bob Abrams, publicity and program director,

booked a variety of new promotions for 1959. "The disk jockey program is one way the Guenther management is appealing to the young set since concession games were ruled out," reported *Billboard.* "In addition to the Ford show, the park's traditional band concerts have been omitting waltz, polka and march tunes and concentrating on a swingier popular fare."

The National Bachelors Organization sponsored an "accent on beauty" contest twice monthly to find the most beautiful girl in America, the typical "Miss Bachelorette." On Father's Day, New Jersey's dad with the largest brood was invited to the park as management's guest. In August the young aerialist Mae West took one look at and exclaimed: "Boy! you really can swing, can't you!" made an appearance on the outdoor stage. "Mr. Sensation" reflected a "new look in aerial artistry," with an act featuring exciting drops, unexpected plunges, a cha-cha routine and a surprise ending.

Robert Guenther, who served as vice president of the National Association of Amusement Parks in 1959-1960, was as ingenious as his father in dream-

146

ABOVE — *The annual Baby Parade stops in front of the judges' stand.* BELOW — *Milton Sonnabend's stand near Fascination, featuring lamps, clocks, radios and cutlery.*

ABOVE — *Entrance to the boat ride as seen from the ramp.* BELOW — *The Dipsy-Doodle, a walk-through fun house.*

ABOVE — *The Tumble Bug, with 40th St. gate at rear.* BELOW — *A ride on the Caterpillar was just the thing on a hot day.*

ABOVE — *A bumper sticker.* BELOW — *A stirring moment is captured forever as Bubbles Riccardo sings the Star-Spangled Banner.*

Gypsy fortune tellers were a part of Olympic's fare as early as 1917 when Madame Stanley set up shop in a dark corner of the dance hall. She was followed by Lady Clark, who held sway during the Thirties and Forties. Were they really gypsies? Most people including park insiders thought so. Their flowing dark-hued costumes, mysterious crystal ball and outlandish gold earings made them look like anything but residents of Vaux Hall, where they actually lived and told fortunes off season. "Madame Wilhelmina had a crystal ball all right," remembers one old-timer, "but she never used it. She read palms and must have been pretty good at her trade. She had hundreds of regular customers and each day, when her stand opened, there was an impatient line waiting outside."

Olympic Park opened its 1961 season on May 6 and 7 with 50,000 visitors. "Birthday time and the season's opening coincided for Olympic Park," re-

Bubbles Riccardo

ing up new park attractions. In June 1960, he announced that school children receiving an "A" in any final subject (except "sittin and starin") would be admitted free to the park. Later that season, he introduced "Teen-o-Rama," a free weekly charm fair for young girls from 12 to 16 under the direction of Marnee Steffens. After a course in carriage, personality and wardrobe, the girls adjourned to the circus grounds where Captain Schreiber's trained chimps marched to the music of the movie, "The Bridge Over the River Kwai." A year later, Guenther began a talent competition at pool side for local teenagers, with weekly eliminations and finals in August.

Wednesdays remained ticket day, when youngsters by the thousands flooded the park clutching long strips of tickets distributed by such well-known firms as Tastee Bread, Mrs. Wagner's Pies, Pepsi Cola, Dugan's Bakery and Fisher Brothers Bakery.

The year 1960 saw the retirement of Madame Helen Smith, who had read palms in a stand behind the Whip near Kiddieland for a decade. Madame Smith was succeeded by her daughter, Madame Wilhelmina Smith, who was to tell fortunes at a dollar a glimpse until the park closed.

ported *Amusement Business.* "The installation celebrated a double observance: 46 years under Guenther family management, and 46 years of age for its president Bob Guenther. Guenther and his brother, Henry Jr., were quick to take advantage of the promotional possibilities. They made it dime day for all rides. And, in addition, anyone proving he had the same birthday as Bob Guenther had free run of the park all day."

Olympic upped its gate price a nickel in 1961 to a modest 20 cents. The year 1961 also brought the return of Allen Durling as publicity agent for the park. City editor of the Elizabeth *Daily Journal,* Durling had been with the park 20 years before leaving in 1957. Together with Karl W. Davey of Fanwood, Durling ran the advertising, press relations and publicity until the park closed.

Changing public tastes cut sharply into the park's attendance during the early Sixties. Although rumors that Olympic would be sold were common, to the annoyance of the concessionaires the Guenthers were close-mouthed about the future. The 1962 season opened on May 26 with several hundred children from Newark's St. Peter's Orphanage as guests of the park and the American Legion. At the circus, top billing went to the Egony Brothers, Danish trapeze stars "who defy death in pirate costumes." Sharing the stage that year were a chimpanzee act from Ecuador; the Kayarts, acrobatic jugglers; musical clowns from England; the Four Haney Girls, acrobats; and the Williams Twins, who performed trampoline tricks high atop a 40-foot pole. The park's brass band was now under the direction of drummer Clem Basile, Captain Joe's nephew. Concerts were at 3, 5:30, 8:30 and 11p.m. Two new rides were installed, the Flying Cages and the Flying Coaster.

Trapeze stars, trained seals named Smaxie and

Olympic Park is closed for the season in this wintertime view looking to the northeast. To the far left, Springfield Avenue.

151

ABOVE — *The annual spring clean-up when everything was given a fresh coat of paint.* BELOW — *Ed Ball paints the Kiddieland fence just before opening day.*

ABOVE — *The picnic grove, bandstand and roller rink, from a postcard.* BELOW — *"The Largest Merry-Go-Round in America."*

153

Maxie and jugglers cavorted for the crowds when the park's 48th season under Guenther management opened in May 1963. In June, the 2,500-seat circus arena (2,000 free bleacher seats and 500 in the grandstand where admission was a dime for kids, 20 cents for adults) echoed to the sounds of the Basile band and the applause of the crowds as the Goetschis, a father-mother-son cycling act, defied the laws of gravity 50 feet above the grass. "Papa Goetschi does the unicycling, with mama riding on his shoulders," said the paper, "and junior sits on hers, playing a violin." Other acts that year

duced to a dime, still drew the crowds. Mondays in August were bargain days, with all rides half price. In June, Hans O. Siepermann of Union was named chief of Olympic Park's 22-man special police force.

New shows, the year's final 10-cent day, fireworks and concerts were crowded into the last two weeks of the season. The final week's circus featured a trapeze act; French poodles; a unicycle act; Happy Davis, a Swedish clown on the trampoline; Hodgini's dog and pony comedy; and the Raymosas, billed as a "Mexican trio in an aerial iron jaw performance." The park rang down the curtain on Labor Day with

Three aspirants for the Miss New Jersey crown — left to right, Maryann Shutz, Gerry Binder and Patricia Morrison — reach for the traditional brass ring, June 17, 1959.

included the Tuckers, comedy trampolinists; Michele and Michael, trapeze stars; Betty Pasco, "a blonde who swings from a chandelier;" the Mephistos, three Egyptian tumblers; Natal, who dressed like an animal; and the inevitable but lovable dog and pony act, this one put through its paces by Alberto Zoppe.

The Miss Olympic Park contests continued at pool side while in the grove the park's 47th annual baby parade wound its way past the judges' stand led by Basile's Olympic Park Band. Ten-cent days, with admission, parking, refreshments and all rides re-

the traditional fireworks display.

A decade of rumor that Olympic Park would be sold to developers became a reality soon after the start of the 1964 season, when plans were unveiled for a $15 million complex of three 21-story luxury apartment towers on the site. Purchase price of the land was said to be nearly $2 million. On July 9, principals of the Kratter Corp., the Guenther family and officials from Irvington and Maplewood gathered in Newark for a luncheon when a mystery caller, later identified only as "a ranking Irvington

ABOVE — *Waiting to board the Merry-Go-Round.* BELOW — *The Merry-Go-Round's fabulous band organ, made in Italy.*

ABOVE — *The Midway from the ramp, looking toward the circus grounds, c. 1960. A row of trees shaded park patrons.*
BELOW — *Basile's band leads the Baby Parade.*

Bubbles Riccardo and Captain Basile

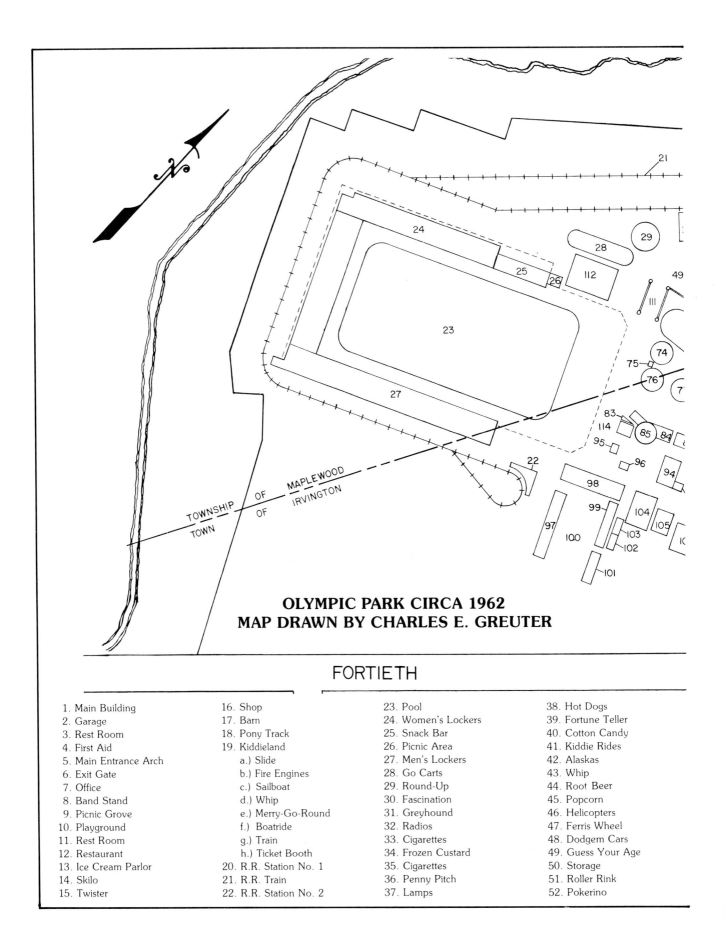

OLYMPIC PARK CIRCA 1962
MAP DRAWN BY CHARLES E. GREUTER

FORTIETH

1. Main Building	16. Shop	23. Pool	38. Hot Dogs
2. Garage	17. Barn	24. Women's Lockers	39. Fortune Teller
3. Rest Room	18. Pony Track	25. Snack Bar	40. Cotton Candy
4. First Aid	19. Kiddieland	26. Picnic Area	41. Kiddie Rides
5. Main Entrance Arch	a.) Slide	27. Men's Lockers	42. Alaskas
6. Exit Gate	b.) Fire Engines	28. Go Carts	43. Whip
7. Office	c.) Sailboat	29. Round-Up	44. Root Beer
8. Band Stand	d.) Whip	30. Fascination	45. Popcorn
9. Picnic Grove	e.) Merry-Go-Round	31. Greyhound	46. Helicopters
10. Playground	f.) Boatride	32. Radios	47. Ferris Wheel
11. Rest Room	g.) Train	33. Cigarettes	48. Dodgem Cars
12. Restaurant	h.) Ticket Booth	34. Frozen Custard	49. Guess Your Age
13. Ice Cream Parlor	20. R.R. Station No. 1	35. Cigarettes	50. Storage
14. Skilo	21. R.R. Train	36. Penny Pitch	51. Roller Rink
15. Twister	22. R.R. Station No. 2	37. Lamps	52. Pokerino

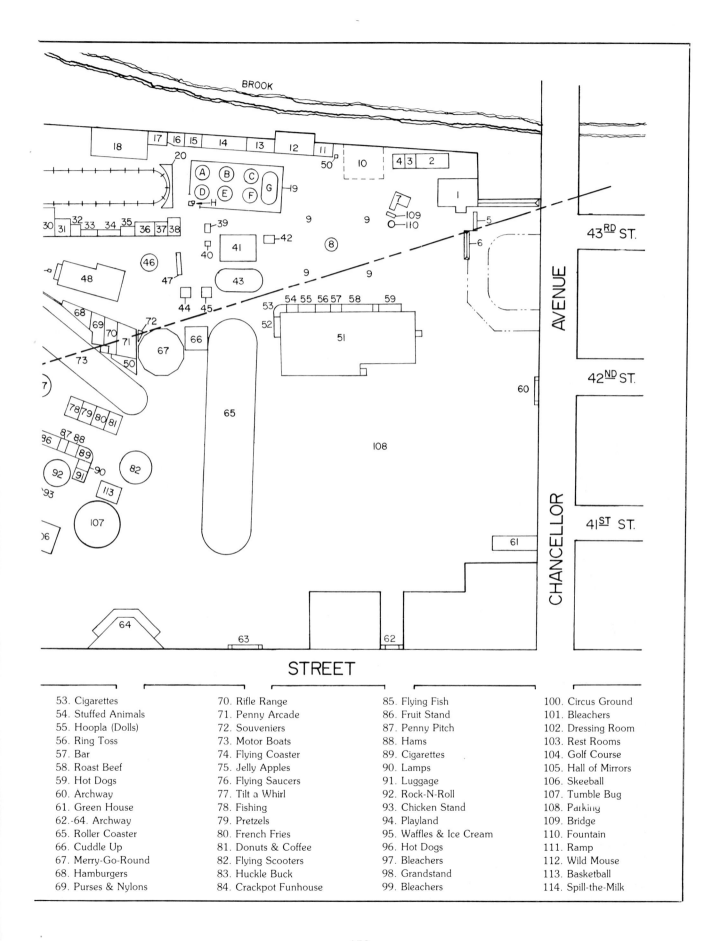

BROOK

43RD ST.

42ND ST.

41ST ST.

AVENUE

CHANCELLOR

STREET

53. Cigarettes	70. Rifle Range	85. Flying Fish	100. Circus Ground
54. Stuffed Animals	71. Penny Arcade	86. Fruit Stand	101. Bleachers
55. Hoopla (Dolls)	72. Souveniers	87. Penny Pitch	102. Dressing Room
56. Ring Toss	73. Motor Boats	88. Hams	103. Rest Rooms
57. Bar	74. Flying Coaster	89. Cigarettes	104. Golf Course
58. Roast Beef	75. Jelly Apples	90. Lamps	105. Hall of Mirrors
59. Hot Dogs	76. Flying Saucers	91. Luggage	106. Skeeball
60. Archway	77. Tilt a Whirl	92. Rock-N-Roll	107. Tumble Bug
61. Green House	78. Fishing	93. Chicken Stand	108. Parking
62.-64. Archway	79. Pretzels	94. Playland	109. Bridge
65. Roller Coaster	80. French Fries	95. Waffles & Ice Cream	110. Fountain
66. Cuddle Up	81. Donuts & Coffee	96. Hot Dogs	111. Ramp
67. Merry-Go-Round	82. Flying Scooters	97. Bleachers	112. Wild Mouse
68. Hamburgers	83. Huckle Buck	98. Grandstand	113. Basketball
69. Purses & Nylons	84. Crackpot Funhouse	99. Bleachers	114. Spill-the-Milk

159

One of the park's many billboards, c. 1965

public official," telephoned a warning that Irvington was about to change the park's zoning from high-rise to garden apartments. Just moments before Robert and Henry Guenther were to sign the deal, the sale was postponed. Despite repeated denials by Irvington officialdom that any zoning change was contemplated, negotiations between Kratter and the Guenthers came to a standstill.

Olympic Park closed for the 1964 season on Sept. 7, its future uncertain. "Amusement Area End Rumored," headlined the Newark *News'* story of the park's final day:

"At 11:30 last night, to the strains of 'September Song' from the covered bandstand in the beer garden, Olympic Park officially closed its gates for the season—and perhaps forever. Although park president Robert Guenther said he still saw no reason why the park wouldn't reopen next year, there was an air of nostalgia when the ferris wheel rocked to a halt and the giant roller coaster discharged its final passenger."

"Perhaps for the first time, it was the old folks, not the youngsters who hung back and were reluctant to take those last few steps through the big, gaily painted iron gates at closing time. Unlike the kids, the grandfathers in shirtsleeves and the grandmothers in print house dresses weren't quite sure if the beer garden with its little white tables, would be there next spring."

The concessionaires met the traditional Labor Day closing with mixed emotions. "The young fellow jerking soda said he'd probably work at the Shore next year if the park didn't reopen. In contrast, most of the old timers were optimistic. The old fellow in

the gray striped apron at the rifle range was certain he'd reopen as he loaded a .22 and collected another quarter. The burly cop keeping an eye on a swarming crowd said he'd be on the beat next summer. He said no one would pay what the park was worth and cited the merry-go-round with its hand-carved wooden horses. The boys in Clem Basile's band were optimistic, too."

Guenther and his wife walked through the park, joined by their son, Robert Jr., for a ride on the roller coaster. Afterward, Guenther paused alone in the beer garden where the park began and discussed the future. "This could be the last year," he said with a smile, "or it could be just another Labor Day closing. A year ago, we tore down a greenhouse in the parking lot and built an expensive fence. This past spring we spent $20,000 on paint as a part of our annual maintenance."

"By midnight, the yells and screams of ageless youth and the rumble and roar of the rides had faded," continued the *News*. "At the pool, the bathers had long since folded their blankets and only a dim string of lights illuminated one of the largest pools in the East. In the shadow of the towering roller coaster, the 'largest merry-go-round in America' had bedded down for the season, its brightly painted ponies silent in the evening's stillness."

Park aficienados gained a reprieve on April 1965 when it was announced that Olympic Park would reopen as usual. "Next Sunday the park gates will open for the 50th season that almost never came," reported the *News*, adding that Guenther had spent the winter "fixing up things and shopping for new

ABOVE — *Three-year-old Susan Claffey at Kiddieland, 1959.* BELOW — *Julius Schwartz owned the U-Drive Boats, Merry Mixer and Wild Mouse.*

ABOVE — *The Brass Band King and his band on the steps of the Irvington Municipal Building.* BELOW — *An aerial view looking southeast, from a postcard.*

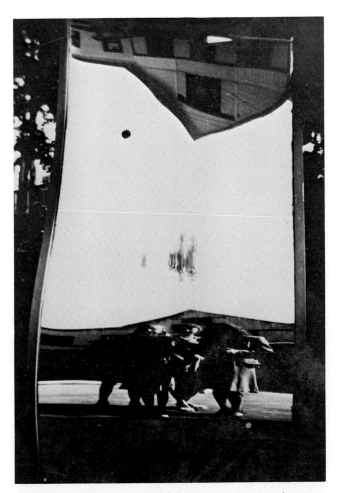

ABOVE — *There were 8 of these mirrors near the main gate.* BELOW — *The roller rink remained open after the season ended.*

rides."

"Inside, workman have started dusting off the merry-go-round, pruning the trees in the beer grove, washing down the roller-coaster and getting the rides and games in order."

"Guenther has also discovered new forms of motion: a 'trabant' that spins people on a tilting turntable; fat little locomotives to take children past a moving mechanical cow; a 'paratrooper' that bounces them up and down, and a 35-foot high 'sky-ride' that Guenther admits is 'much smaller than the one at the World's Fair, but at least it returns riders to the starting point.' The roller coaster, the carrousel with the hand-carved horses and calliope, U-drive boats and gigantic swimming pool are still there, though someone has yet to turn on the faucets for the 10-day pool filling operation. About the only casualty over the winter were the unsuccessful 'air saucers' of the last season that floated on a cushion of air. 'You just can't tell how some rides will go,' Guenther laughed. 'The grown-ups just didn't have the patience to steer the saucers and they didn't go fast enough for the kids.'"

What would eventually prove to be Olympic's last season got off to a lively—and discouraging—start on May 1 when a crowd of 400 to 500 youths from Newark went on a rampage inside the park, wrecking amusement machines and stealing prizes. Chased out the gates, they spilled over into neighboring residential areas, smashing windows and terrorizing pedestrians in a wild melee that grabbed headlines and frightened away patrons.

The balance of the park's 50th season under Guenther family management was quieter, with tens of thousands enjoying the pool, band concerts and fireworks. Kiddieland, with its slide, fire engines, sail boat, Whip and train continued to do a good business. The pony track, go-carts, speed boats, fortune teller, dude ranch, Whip, Ferris Wheel, Dodgem cars, Rock n' Roll, penny arcade, Cuddle Up, Octopus, funhouse and a host of other rides and attractions still provided enjoyment for "children of all ages." Waffles and hot dogs, frozen custard, root beer, jelly apples, pretzels and French fries were sold by the thousands.

Mondays were bargain days, with all rides half price; the popular 10-cent days drew the crowds as they always had. Jack Bilby again broadcast his radio show, "Summer Showcase," on Friday evenings from the music grove. The teen-age social club, Red Cross swim classes in the pool, baby parade and class trips to "one of the few big family resorts left in the metropolitan area" continued as before.

Parking was now free in the 2,000-car lot. In cele-

The roller coaster and motor boats, July 11, 1964.

bration of Olympic's golden jubilee, management offered free admission to anyone 50 years old in 1965. One hopeful sign that the park might remain was the installation of a new and expensive ride called The Skyline. Modelled after a ski tow, the ride transported passengers 1,000 feet on a tour of the park 35 feet above ground. Ed Ball and Henry A. Guenther III owned the new ride.

The Guenthers had cut back the circus to three acts in recent years but even so, the allure of free vaudeville drew good crowds twice daily: Trained Russian wolfhounds; Novelle's original poodle symphony; trapeze artists; perch balancers; jugglers; high wire comics; Doberman pinschers; Lemke's educated chimpanzees; and Allen's three Alaskan bruin bears were among June's star performers. Princess Tajano, a trapeze artist at the N.Y. World's Fair; Tovarisch and Comrades, billed as "dogdom's funniest troupe;" trained seals, collies and bears; a

troupe from Australia's back country adept at rope spinning and whip cracking; and The Great Veno, the "world's premiere wire walker," who walked a wire angled at 45 degrees, enthralled park patrons. The free circus for the closing week of the jubilee season featured Bob and Lauren Top, who roller skated on a 6-foot circular platform atop a 60-foot flagpole; Lona Antelek and Her Canines; and Leo Gasca, a Mexican tight wire performer. The Park closed its gates on Sept. 6 amid rumors that its 79th season, 50 of them under Guenther management, would be its last.

On Sept. 23, 1965, Robert Guenther made the fatal announcement: A new buyer had been found, he said, and even if the sale did not materialize the park would never reopen.

"From the outside it looks like the end of just another season," wrote a Maplewood *News-Record* reporter who visited the park in October. "The big

In the Sixties the old airplane swing was updated with Bill Tracy-made fish bodies.

Emcee Bob Guenther studies the program before an afternoon circus performance.

Bob Guenther tries out the paratrooper ride as Fred Bellina stands ready to paint, May 1965.

'Smile' sign still hangs there, ready to welcome more of the millions who have passed under it. And the old bandstand remains under a shady grove of trees where generations of visitors have relaxed. But appearances are deceptive at Olympic Park. Inside, many of the rides and games have been ripped down and shipped to entertainment sites in various parts of the nation. The disassembling process has been going on for about a month now and it signals the end of the Irvington-Maplewood landmark. Owners Robert A. and Henry A. Guenther Jr. aren't ready to say the park has actually been sold for a reported $2 million, but they state flatly that the season ended on Labor Day was their last—that Olympic will never open again. For the two brothers, the park's closing means more than the end of an era, it closes out a life's work."

Robert reminisced awhile with the reporter, recalling the music of John Philip Sousa, the midget auto racing, the Mardi Gras "and the time the man-buried-alive ran up such a fantastic telephone bill in his below-the-ground box that his concessionaire boss had to cut off his phone service." Most of all, though, he remembered the people. "You would walk through the park on a warm and sunny day and see people enjoy themselves," he said.

Over the years, said Guenther, Olympic Park "basically remained the same." Unlike most other amusement parks, for instance, Olympic always kept its bandstand. "It wasn't the attraction it used to be," he said of the last few years. "But we kept it mostly for the circus; it makes a much better show than playing records."

"Some of the rides and games changed, though. 'Tastes have changed,' said Guenther. 'The youngsters today are more sophisticated, more blase. They require more thrills. Where once it was the biggest thrill in a kid's life to ride the merry-go-round,

166

today's breed wants even bigger thrills: the roller coaster, the Whip, the bumper cars, the Flying Scooter, the Bug.'"

"Why is Olympic closing? 'There's no basic reason,' said Guenther. But rising land values are part of it. And there were a number of operating problems, he said. Also he had lost some of his old enthusiasm in recent years."

"A small maintenance crew remains at the park. There's still roller skating at Olympic, and the rides and games have to be kept in shape until they're sold. But the grounds are deserted, except for an occasional concessionaire come to putter around his property. John Mineo, operator for 10 years of the Flying Scooter, looked across the park and remembered how people loved that ride. 'We were busy every minute,' he said. 'The people didn't want to get off.' He paused a moment, looking over the stripped-down steel arms of the scooter ride. 'This was a nice place to work,' he said. 'I feel sad.'"

Olympic Park was to remain empty and overgrown for 13 years until 1979, when construction began on a light industrial park on the site.

"Olympic Park has yielded at last to changing time and taste," said the Newark *News* in September 1965, after the park closed. "Surviving long after it had become an anachronism, it was the last of many amusement parks, large and small, which once furnished Essex County with much of its summer time recreation. . . ."

"The early parks were decorous, inexpensive and family-centered, with leafy groves, unpretentious gardens and many places to sit down. It was no coincidence in the pre-motor age that each was built at the end of a trolley line equipped in summer with

The Merry-Go-Round's handcarved horses are prepared for the long journey west.

open cars. . . ."

"A generation that can be diverted by nothing less than a Disneyland accepts their oblivion with equanimity. But those who remember childhood, spent in that slower, quieter and less affluent era brush a nostalgic tear."

16

CHERISHED MEMORIES

How many people remember Olympic Park today, 18 years after it closed? There's no way of telling, although the number must be in the hundreds of thousands. One thing is certain — the park may be gone now but it has not been forgotten, and its memory will remain bright for a good many years to come.

Stop Trying to Steer that Horse!

"During the First World War my family moved from Mendham to Newark," recalls Willard A. Burnett, now of Livingston. "In Mendham, we always looked forward to the annual visit of the travelling carnival, and we missed that great fun when we came to Newark. Then we found out about Olympic Park."

"I can remember as a boy of 12 climbing aboard an open trolley car, hanging on the steps as long as we were allowed, and getting off at Olympic Park. Sometimes we joined a Sunday School picnic, at other times we were part of a family outing. We were poor, so we had to make the most of a few rides on the merry-go-round, roller coaster or one or two other amusements. We were amazed when our father and mother joined

us on those rides: We thought they were far too old to withstand the excitement."

"When we lived in the country I had ridden farm horses in from the fields, so I knew my way around animals. One day I bought a ticket for the pony ride, then located near the roller coaster. As we cantered around the track, my horse refused to follow my directions and I complained to the attendant. 'Stop trying to steer the horse,' he said, as he threw the reins over the animal's head, hitting it on the rump. My horse took off with a start and when he reached an opening in the fence, trotted under the roller coaster and galloped over to a track on the far side. Eventually, I seized the reins and brought him back. The attendant wanted to charge me extra for that ride, but I refused to pay, saying it was his fault."

"Sometime later, I went to a dance at Olympic Park, my first. I remember putting my arm around a girl and the

embarrassment when I touched the lacing of her corset: How times have changed."

Flouncy Dresses and White Buckskin Shoes

"Life in Irvington in the Twenties and early Thirties was typically small-town despite the building boom then underway," writes Marie Cahill Cooney, who still lives there. "Few families owned automobiles, but trolley-car and train connections made an occasional boat ride up the Hudson River or a trip to Coney Island or the Jersey Shore possible. More often, however, Olympic Park was the focus of our recreational activities."

"Preparations for our weekly visit to the park included Sunday-best dress-up. Father wore his blue serge suit with white shirt and tie and his straw skimmer, purchased anew each year. We girls wore white, flouncy dresses made by mother, with tucks and lace insertions and wide pink or blue satin sashes and bows. Mother also insisted that we wear white stockings and white buckskin shoes, which we were expected somehow to keep clean. There was a dignified tone about the park in those days, and visitors dressed in their finest outfits. With baby brother propped up on pillows in his express wagon, the family walked the dirt and gravel paths (sidewalks had not been installed yet) a few short blocks to the park. Because we lived within earshot of the park's noises, we had free seasonal passes."

"For us children, Olympic Park was a wonderful fairyland. To our parents, who had spent many an evening while courting at performances by the Aborn Opera Co., it brought back nostalgic memories. I have a clear recollection that just inside the gate there seemed to be a sharp drop in temperature even on the hottest days. The overlapping canopy of tree branches looked skyhigh to me; so different were they from trees anywhere else that they were always a source of wonder. At the entrance were colorful displays of carefully cultivated flowers that changed with the seasons."

"Our first stop was always the full-length funny mirrors that distorted and contorted so delightfully. Next came the tantilizing aroma of hamburgers and onions, frankfurters, caramel pop-corn, cotton candy, roasting peanuts, waffles, ice cream and Peters chocolates. Since we had just eaten dinner, mother and father turned deaf ears to our pleas, heading us instead straight back to the circus where high-wire walkers, gymnasts, jugglers and animal acts put on a hair-raising show."

"And now came the rides and games. Depending on our ages, we rode the roller coaster, ponies, Whip, merry-go-round, Dodgem or Ferris Wheel or played a variety of skill games. The sounds of machinery bumping and crashing mingled with the calliope music to drown out all conversation. Sight, sound and smell created a delightful world from which we left reluctantly. Only the promise of food could persuade us to move on."

"The picnic tables and benches near the bandstand were always crowded. Munching a hot dog smothered with mustard and drinking root beer, we sat still (for a time at least) while our parents enjoyed a fine band concert."

"After the concert we walked toward the games of chance. We considered our father a master: We knew he was the one person the chance operators preferred not to see. He would stand awhile watching the spinning wheels, figure out the pattern and finally put down a nickel or a dime. Nine times out of 10, he would win a basket of groceries, or sugar or coffee, a smoked ham, bacon and eggs, leather goods, a clock or a watch, a canary in a cage, kewpie dolls (some dressed in feathered head-dresses with hula skirts that wiggled), boxes of chocolate candy and on and on. Burdened with prizes, our stomachs full, exhausted from the rides, we were at last ready to leave Olympic Park for another week. Only on those nights when fireworks were shown was the routine varied. Then, we arrived after supper and stayed late to enjoy the display. Of all my childhood memories, those Sundays at Olympic Park a half-century ago remain vivid still."

Never Really Away from Olympic Park

Viola Bertelin of Mansfield, La., spent her pre-teen years in a beautiful old house a mile or so from the park. "It was the greatest of treats when our parents took us to Olympic Park on a summer Sunday to spend the day."

"In the early Twenties, when I was a small child of seven or eight, I had my first popsicle at Olympic Park. They were so different from today's commercial pops, for they were made with real orangeade; orange, incidentally, was the only flavor. The man who sold the popsicles froze them right before your eyes, pouring the orangeade into glass cylinders that looked like oversized test tubes. They cost five cents and were they delicious."

"The funny mirrors set up against the old trees were an endless source of fascination and delight. They were the first things we rushed to when we arrived, and the last we visited upon leaving."

"Each summer Three Cent Day was set aside for the children when the price of all rides was only three cents. My sisters and I went one time, but never again. The crowds were unbelievable, and the waiting lines so long it took away all the fun."

"I remember Lucky Lotto, now called Bingo. People played on Bingo-type cards, but instead of BINGO, the letters on the cards spelled out LUCKY. Chicken corn kernels were used as markers. The players, most of them men, sat in chairs built upon tiers similar to bleachers, each playing a card held in his lap. The caller would intone K-54 and a chorus of voices would repeat in unison, K-54. My father, who sometimes played, won lovely baskets of fruit."

"There were many wheels of fortune, but we children never felt we could squander our few pennies on those; instead, we played the string pull, a game where you selected a string from a handful held by the attendant. All of the strings were ostensibly attached to gorgeous prizes, such as dolls and skates, with a great many insignificant items scattered in between. I never won nor did I ever see anyone else win one of the beautiful prizes, but we had the joy of believing we might—and we did always get something in return for our investment, no matter how small—a comb, a small picture frame, once even a rainbow glass dish I gave to my mother."

"After I married I always found time to visit Olympic Park. On my husband's day off, a group of us would pack a lunch and spend the day at the pool, a cool and lovely spot, and extremely well kept."

"In 1945, when my children were small, my husband was transferred to South Jersey. We had a longing to see the park again and, in 1964, took a ride up with our son and his new wife. They had a chance to enjoy the place where we had spent so many happy days, to ride on the World's Biggest Merry-Go-Round, and to stand in front of those dear mirrors, still leaning up against those magnificent old trees. Although it had been almost 20 years, it seemed for those few hours that we had never really been away from Olympic Park."

On the Good Ship Olympic

"There I was, all of 14 years old, decked out in feathers and bows for

'Swing, Mr. Charlie,' one of the production numbers in our 1936 show, 'The Good Ship Olympic,'" writes Miriam Hull. "We all belonged to Lillian Daniels' School of the Dance in those days, and how I loved it. Every summer we put on a free show at Olympic Park, at first in the band shell where Joe Basile's band played and later at the circus grounds."

"Those were the best of times: No war, no violence. Despite the Depression, everything was just wonderful, at least for a teenager at Olympic Park. I enjoyed my first kiss in the Old Mill and took my first dive in the waters of the pool. There will never be a hot roast beef sandwich as tasty as those at the park and, oh boy, how I remember those waffles with ice cream and the hot dogs loaded with mustard, relish and sauerkraut. And how can I ever forget the open-air trolleys that deposited you right at the park's gate—heaven help you if a sudden summer shower came along, for your only protection was a sometimes very balky canvas shade that pulled down. But even a rainshower failed to dampen my enthusiasm. How I enjoyed the rides (especially on the days we gave our show, when they were free), and the games, the prizes, the food and of course our shows, when we danced to such tunes as 'Sugar Blues,' 'Take a Number from One to Ten,' 'Saint Louis Blues,' 'The Sheik of Araby,' and 'Lilac Time.'"

"I'm so glad I can look back on those days at Olympic Park. Today's youth simply cannot know what they missed. Olympic was a vital part of my youth; when it closed, I was heart-broken. Sometimes, when I think the world has changed too much, too fast, I sit a while remembering those bygone days at Olympic Park, grateful for the warm memories I'll cherish forever.

Jack the Ripper and an Ancient Mummy

"I remember Olympic Park as a place where the whole family could enjoy itself," recalls Lorraine Chesek of Port Monmouth, who grew up in Newark during the Forties and Fifties.

"I'll never forget those clown faces on the gates, enticing you to enter. And once you went inside, you left the big city behind for a fantasy world."

"I was a small girl then, holding tightly onto my parents' hands, hypnotized by the sights and sounds. I always looked for the giant wooden roller coaster that loomed up out of the trees, but, though it was the main attraction there, I never had any desire to ride it. The hawkers at the stands intrigued me more. Each one tried to outshout the other for my attention. I would have tried each game, but my parents had strict rules. My favorite was a fishing game where you dragged a small fishing pole with a weight and magnet on the end along the bottom of a water-filled tank. If you were lucky enough to catch a gold fish, you had your choice of prizes. The other fish had numbers on them corresponding with numbered shelves filled with prizes. I never managed to get above the bottom shelf."

"The little power motorboats fascinated me. You could pilot your own boat on the water and around a maze until an attendant with a long hooked pole pulled you to shore, the signal your ride was over. I was never really fond of most of the other rides, though I would attempt two or three regularly. As a rule, I liked to have my feet firmly planted on the ground. My older sister, more adventurous than I, never stopped cajoling me into joining her on all the rides."

"I'll never forget the time my sister coaxed me onto the Octopus. My sister and I and a young soldier and his date shared the car. The ride had barely begun when I started to cry; by the time the ride ended, my head was in the soldier's lap. While he tried vainly to console me, his date just sat there, no doubt wondering what she had done to deserve our company—if you could have called it that. Just once did my cousin and I ride the Caterpillar together. After the ride began, a canvas awning enveloped the cars, making them look like a green caterpillar. My cousin, who knew how I felt about rides in general, glowed as she told me how black widow spiders nested in the folds of the canvas, ready to drop down on unsuspecting riders."

"My two favorite rides were the merry-go-round and the Dude Ranch, which featured huge but harmless mechanical horses with stupid painted grins on their faces. Once you were seated inside, the horse became a bucking bronco as it rode along a track."

"Near the pool was the snow cone concession, my favorite. On a hot day, nothing tasted better or cooled me off faster than a snow cone topped with flavored syrup. Nearby was the circus. My parents always treated us to a show whenever we visited Olympic Park. Just before taking our seats, my father would buy some French fries and a soda for everyone. The circus band played before and during the acts, which, by the way, were very good, especially the acrobats, jugglers, trained dogs and magicians."

"After the circus we went back to the stands and past the fun house where giant faces leered at the crowds and weird laughter made me jump. As a small child, I admired the bravery of those who went inside: I never joined them. Occasionally, though, I did visit the wax museum, gazing in astonishment at Jack the Ripper and an ancient Indian mummy in a glass case. He was, I thought, very well preserved indeed. I also enjoyed trying to win a goldfish by tossing ping pong balls into a bowl. Believe you me, the day I won that prize I strutted proud as a peacock through the crowds, the goldfish bowl under my arm. Later in the day, I would try to find time to parade back and forth in front of the trick mirrors near the main gate, giggling outrageously as I grew by turns fat and thin, tall and short."

"As the evening drew to a close, we retraced our steps to the bandstand and the picnic tables and benches nearby where people enjoyed a late night snack before heading home. My father bought hot roast beef sandwiches and I looked forward to this special time with my family when we visited the park."

Stop this Thing! I Want to Get Off!

Olympic Park closed when Linda Slifkin of Maplewood was only 11 years old. "I was so very sad. I missed the park for a long time afterwards; my fondest childhood memories were of the park, memories I cherish to this day." Linda's favorite bedtime story, repeated again and again by her father, was "Bracelet and Necklace," the continuing saga of a fun-loving couple who visited the park regularly. "To this day I don't know which was the boy and which was the girl; it didn't matter to me. I loved them because Bracelet and Necklace loved the park as much as I did. The only difference was that they always rode the roller coaster and I was too scared to dare it."

"The roller coaster was the park's main attraction for me. It was the largest structure I had ever seen; it dominated the park, and its screaming riders could be heard for miles — or so I imagined. I knew in my heart the day would come when I would summon up my courage and ride the coaster, just as Bracelet and Necklace did. When that time came, I told myself more than once, my little girl days would be over."

"The delicious anticipation of *someday* marching up to the roller coaster's ticket taker never kept me from enjoying the less frightening attractions at Olympic Park. My favorite was the donkey ride. With every loud hee-haw, the animal rocked forward and backward, round and round, on its track. What a delightful way to work up an appetite. Two rounds on the lifelike donkey and I was ready for cotton candy and popcorn, two of my favorites. Nothing could and ever will compare in my mind with that pink fluffy candy or the salty, buttered popcorn my father always bought me."

"Playing games for prizes was a regular treat. The first booth I ran to after my father and I entered the park was the one where I learned all I ever cared to know about fishing. The attendant handed me a wooden stick with a string and metal hook at the end. The deep, murky waters of the tank swallowed my hook and I remember standing for what seemed like hours until I got a bite. One memorable night, I won four stackable ashtrays for catching a small fish. Weekends were special during the spring and summer because invariably, if I had been a good girl, my reward was an outing to Olympic Park."

"As time passed I could stall the inevitable no longer: Bracelet and Necklace beckoned me. My father held my hand tightly as we finally approached the roller coaster, bought our tickets, sat down in the compartment and pulled the shiny silver protective bar close to our chests. As prepared for the moment as I thought I was, it had never occurred to me that the roller coaster wouldn't stop if one small frightened girl wanted to get off. Less than halfway up the track, I lost my nerve. 'I want to get off,' I cried, over and over. 'Stop this thing.' My stomach did flip-flops. My father tried to comfort me but I cried even harder, convinced I would never live to hear another bedtime story. I don't really know what came over me. I do remember never wanting to hear about Bracelet and Necklace again as I staggered off the roller coaster for the first and last time in my life. No one, not even my father, had told me growing up was going to be so terrifying."

We Emphasized the Family Aspect

"I have a flood of memories about the place," wrote Allen Durling, who handled the park's publicity in the Forties and Fifties and again from 1961 to 1965. "The thing we emphasized, fairly successfully I think, was the family aspect. The summer's biggest event probably was the baby parade with three prizes given in four categories, blondes, redheads, brunets and best floats. We got a big press play on this, hustling pictures to the Sunday papers and the hometown press of the winning tots."

"My personal heartache was the fact that Olympic Park was larger than Palisades Park, yet the latter's larger budget for promotion and its proximity to Manhattan, left unchallenged *its* claim to be greater."

"The swimming pool was huge and the site of meets, as well as the place for my photographers to prowl for 'cheesecake' which, hopefully, we could place in the New York tabloids or the wire services."

"The management was a family affair. Son Robert helped in the office, Henry Jr. was an 'outside' man. In-laws, a family named Fuchs, had prominent roles. Albert E. Fuchs, Mary Guenther's brother, was the office manager; Leonard Fuchs of Maplewood handled all the park's insurance, a pretty big job."

"Three free outdoor acts, after-noons and evenings, were a daily attraction. These were booked through the George Hamid agency and usually comprised an animal act, an aerial show such as a swaypole, and an interim act which could be jugglers, roller skaters or what have you. After so many of them, I dread even today the thought of another trained dog act."

After retiring as city editor of the *Daily Journal* in 1967, Durling moved to Florida where he worked as an editor at the *Sentinel Star* in Orlando. "Imagine my glee when Walt Disney World was established and gave a place of honor to Olympic's old merry-go-round. Naturally enough, I did a big feature story about it."

The Finest Park of Them All

Theresa Clancy of Kearny "cried a little" when Olympic Park closed its doors in 1965. "From 1921 to 1923 I lived in a house overlooking the park from whose windows I enjoyed an unobstructed view of much of the activity there all summer long. Visitors from Newark and points south and north rode the Springfield Avenue trolley marked '43rd Street' or 'Olympic Park' directly to the entrance. After discharging their passengers, the trolleys looped around a beautiful flower bed, then returned to the city for another load. It was quite a pastime just to watch trolley after trolley deposit fun-seekers at the park's gate every 10 minutes or so. When the weather was suitable, open-air trolleys were placed into service. Behind the trolley loop ran a long fence to the rear of which the circus acts were sheltered. I loved to peep through holes in the fence to watch the horses and elephants feed on hay. Once in a while I even heard an elephant trumpet, something few 10-year olds today can claim."

"I spent a good deal of my time at the park during summer vacation. You entered through a turnstile where friendly cashiers accepted the admission fee, then walked directly to what I called the magic mirrors where nearly everyone paused to laugh at themselves. Those wonderful mirrors set the tone for the day's activities;

whether they made me tall or short, long-headed or short-legged, skinny or fat or just plain funny, I could have spent all day there."

"Beyond the mirrors to the center and left of the entrance were tables and benches where picnickers ate their lunches or rested while listening to a band concert. I recall John Philip Sousa's band there and can to this day form a mental picture of that great man waving his baton in the air. If you happened to be hungry or thirsty, there were refreshment stands on the left that sold ice cold beer, or soda, root beer, lemonade, ice cream, hamburgers and hot dogs. On a platform near the bandstand, free afternoon and evening shows were presented. The acts changed weekly, and I missed nary a one all summer. Keenly, I watched as aerialists, acrobats, clowns, tumblers, jugglers, trained dogs, dancing horses, trained elephants and tigers on sturdy chains performed. Joe Basile's band accompanied the acts with heart-stirring, foot-tapping music. After the free show, I would sometimes run home, round up my girlfriends and play "showtime."

"Beyond the refreshment stands were booths where you could win prizes. One stand had fancy boxes of candy. At another the customer threw a hoop at prizes stacked on blocks and, if the hoop circled the block, you won the prize. It wasn't easy, I can tell you that. There was also a Go-Fish stand for the children, who tried to hook a fish with a small pole. Each fish had a number corresponding to a prize. At my favorite stand, you placed a dime on your lucky number, then watched as small numbered balls were released from the top of a miniature roller coaster. While the balls raced along the track, you cheered your number toward the finish line. The prize was usually a kewpie doll with blue, green, yellow, pink or red feathers."

"One of the first rides beyond the picnic grove was the Tilt-a-Whirl, which rocked side to side as it spun around. Close to it was the Whip, everybody's favorite. Here too was the Caterpillar, a ride that circled round and round, up and down. When the green canopy closed over the riders, a pleasant draft of cool air came rushing in, much to the embarrassment of the girls who forgot to hold their skirts down. Nearby was the Ferris Wheel—what a thrill it was to be stopped at the top rocking back and forth gently as you gazed down at Olympic Park spread beneath you. After dark the view was breathtaking."

"To the east side of the grounds stood the giant roller coaster, the park's number one thrill ride. From my bedroom window I watched as the cars glided along the track, and listened to the screams of the riders as they dipped suddenly or rounded a sharp curve. Next to the roller coaster was the Old Mill, or tunnel of love, where couples and young children enjoyed a slow boat ride through the dark tunnel. Every few yards a horrible figure would pop out, almost scaring you out of your seat."

"Beside the Old Mill was the large merry-go-round, the grandest ride of them all, enjoyed by children and adults alike. A pipe organ played popular tunes and marches as the gaily-painted horses and chariots spun around. Young children usually sat in the chariots with their parents, but we older youngsters enjoyed the jumping horses best of all. To catch the brass ring and win a free ride was quite an achievement. The wooden benches surrounding the merry-go-round were usually crowded with onlookers who seemed to enjoy the music and laughter as much as did the riders."

"Next in line was the penny arcade, and what fun it was to slip a coin into a slot for pictures of famous actors and actresses, or for cards that pictured our future spouses or children. There was also a 'Grandma' machine that told fortunes, and machines that dispensed small toys or candy if you had skill enough maneuvering a tiny derrick. It was an inexpensive way to spend an enjoyable hour or so. On the sidewalk outside the arcade loomed the 'Test Your Strength' tower. Wives and girlfriends stood back as husbands or boyfriends heaved the bulky hammer down onto the platform, hoping to shoot the ball to the top of the tower and ring the bell. Here also was a man who guessed your weight. If he missed by two pounds or more, you won a small prize. The man also guessed ages, but not too many ladies liked that idea."

"Closer to the center of the park were the kiddie rides. A tiny merry-go-round, little boats, miniature automobiles and a small Whip stand out in my mind. Always filled with laughing, happy children, too, was the little train that ran nearby. The train boasted a run of a mile along the west side of the park, and there was never a lack of passengers waiting to step aboard."

"A shooting range stood near the arcade and across from it were the Dodgem cars, a noisy place where riders took special delight bumping into each other. Honestly, I preferred maneuvering out of the way. Among the stands on the west side was one operated by an Oriental family. The prizes there were hand-painted Japanese scenes, inexpensive then but valuable collector's pieces today. The favorite children's stand was the one where you selected a string from perhaps 20 or so held by the attendant, pulled on it and won whatever prize was attached. Needless to say, among so many strings it was rare to come up with a decent prize, but we didn't much care."

"I returned to Olympic Park as a teenager to swim in the pool or, more often, for the free Monday night ballroom dancing. Years later, after I married, my husband and I brought our youngsters to the park. They loved it every bit as much as I had, and best of all, I had the pleasure of reliving my childhood days at the finest amusement park of them all."

172

INDEX

ACKNOWLEDGMENTS

This book would not have been possible without the cooperation and generous assistance of hundreds of people who contributed photographs, memorabilia and their most cherished memories of Olympic Park. In a very real sense these people are the authors of this work, and I thank them most sincerely: Celeste M. Alleyne, Mrs. Harold Armstrong, Dorothy Banahan, Herbert Baudistel, Alice Behnke, Marilyn Belli, Nancy F. Benner, Viola Bertelin, Henry F. Blank, Norman E. Bobel, Lila Borden, Richard L. Bowker, W. Phillips Brooks, Frank Budney, the Burbella Family, Barbara S. Burke, Willard A. Burnett, Jerry Caprio, Maryann P. Carlowitz, Mrs. John H. Carlson, John M. Caruthers, George Cassidy, Lorraine Chesek, Hedwig Christian, Joseph Claffey, Theresa Clancy, Marie C. Cooney, Albert L. Creamer, John DeLuca, Mrs. F. Demcsak, Mrs. B. Dietze, Allen Durling, William J. Eckert Jr., Theodore Edison, Felix Fox, Esther Y. Frank, Mrs. Harvey Freeman Sr., Frederick Fried, Ethel Gaedenak, Mr. and Mrs. John Gallagher, Edward Gebhard, Ethel Gilles, John Goellner, Lovella N. Goncalves, Catherine Grosso, Henry A. Guenther III, Angelo Giuliano, Sidney Harris, C. Stewart Hausmann, Ida A. Heinemeyer, Otis P. Henry III and family, Richard P. Hock, Marion Hoesley, Danny Hope, Miriam Hull, Florence E. Hunt, Helen B. Hutchinson, Anna Jacobus, William Johnson, Caroline Kauffeld, Mr. and Mrs. Charles B. Kelly, Mr. and Mrs. Paul Klein Jr., Mrs. M. Kobin, Elaine Koehler, John J. Leahy, Edith Lindsay, Thomas Loucopoulous, Mike Martin, Mr. and Mrs. Fred Mazzone, Marie McArthur, Janet H. McDowell, Edna McMunn, Donald McTiernan, Valentine P. Meissner, Jack Mendelsohn, Mr. and Mrs. William Mericle, Gerald E. Miko, Eleanor Minetti, Vincent Minner, Misak K. Murdichian, Claire M. Mykowski, Mr. and Mrs. Raymond Neveil, Joseph H. Palmer Jr., Nancy Paris,

Josephine Pascal, Erna Pflueger, Mrs. Benjamin Quist, Mrs. Joseph Rahner, Herbert Ramo, Marie Renka, Mildred Richardson, Marie Kurz Roberts, Robert R. Roberts, Clinton N. Rutan, Mr. and Mrs. Phil Samuels, Muriel Sargent, Jules Schwartz, Irene Schweitzer, Lorraine Shaffer, George A. Siessel, Herbert J. Singe, Red Skelton, Linda Slifkin, George Sobin Jr., Alice Sockler, Miriam Sodergren, Elsie B. Sonitz, A. Soriano, Fred Spielberger, Lucille Starke, Al Steiner, Helen Stephanie, Elizabeth Stewart, Lillian Tafaro, Philip Timpanaro, Ira G. Tompkins, Sheridan Tortorello, Mildred Urban, Mary Weaver, Clara M. Weferling, Janice C. Wheeler, D. E. Williams, Lillian Woodhead and Robert Yancheck. A special word of appreciation is due to Christine McCloskey, Mr. and Mrs. William Mericle, Mr. and Mrs. Carl J. Perina, Mr. and Mrs. Robert R. Roberts, Marian Schuetz and Mr. and Mrs. George Sobin Jr. Tom and Rudy Petrelli of American Graphic, Inc. were especially helpful during the publication phase of this book. Others who rendered invaluable assistance were: Carl J. Perina, Marian Schuetz, Vida Truesdell, Marion Ritter and Marie C. Cooney, who read nearly a half-century of newspaper files; Henry F. Blank, who processed all of the photos used in this book; Charles E. Greuter, who drew the map appearing on pages 158-159; Christine McCloskey, who proofread the galleys; June S. Mericle, who provided much first-hand information and numerous photographs; Verne Blake, who interviewed a score of people, collected photographs, wrote captions and articles and proofread the manuscript; Marie C. Cooney, whose translations from the German may be found throughout the early chapters; and my wife, BJ, who not only helped with the index but also ageed to share me with this book for two years. I am also indebted to William P. Huber, Vice President, Gannett Outdoor Advertising; Dr. Carl A. Lane, Keeper of Manuscripts, and Kathleen Stavec, Librarian, both of the N.J. Historical Society; Charles W. Cummings and his staff at the Newark Public Library; Samuel H. High III, President, Philadelphia Toboggan Co.; Dr. Ruth Lang of the Irvington High School faculty; and Charles J. Jacques Jr., Editor, *Amusement Park Journal.* Books which proved particularly useful were: *Maplewood Past and Present*, Helen B. Bates, Ed. (1948); *A Pictorial History of the Carousel* by Frederick Fried (1964); *Dime-Store Dream Parade* by Robert Heide and John Gilman (1978); *Amusing the Millions* by John F. Kasson (1978); *The Great American Amusement Parks* by Gary Kyriazi (1976); *The Outdoor Amusement Industry* by William F. Mangels (1952); *Red Skelton* by Arthur Marx (1979); *The German-Americans* by Richard O'Connor (1968); my own book, *Out of Our Past, a History of Irvington, New Jersey* (1974); *A History of the City of Newark, New Jersey*, by Frank J. Urquhart (1913); and *Roller Coaster Fever* by John Waldrop (1979). As might be expected, a great deal of information about Olympic Park was found in old newspaper files, including *The Clinton Weekly*, Elizabeth *Daily Journal*, *Der Erzahler*, Irvington *Herald*, The Irvington *News*, Maplewood *Home News*, Maplewood *News-Record*, Newark *Daily Advertiser*, Newark *Evening News*, Newark *Evening Star*, Newark *Star Eagle*, Newark *Sunday Call*, Newark *Sunday News*, Newark *Tribune*, New Jersey *Deutsche Zeitung*, New Jersey *Frei Zeitung* and The New York *Times*. Articles about the park in *Amusement Business*, *Amusement News*, *Amusement Park Journal*, *Amusement Park Management*, *Billboard*, *Dog House*, *Olympic Park Marathon News*, *Olympic Park Rink News* and *New Jersey Monthly* were also consulted. Other sources were: Irvington Township License Bureau and Department of Public Works; Register of Deeds and Surrogate of Essex County, New Jersey; Clinton Cemetery Association, Irvington; and an excellent unpublished manuscript by Margery Selden entitled, "Opera on the Trolley Line."